Marriage: From Surviving to Thriving
Workbook

Marriage: From Surviving to Thriving
Workbook

BASED ON THE BOOK BY

CHARLES R. SWINDOLL

Produced in association with CREATIVE MINISTRIES
Insight for Living

W PUBLISHING GROUP
A Division of Thomas Nelson Publishers
Since 1798

www.wpublishinggroup.com

MARRIAGE: FROM SURVIVING TO THRIVING
WORKBOOK

Published by W Publishing Group, a division of Thomas Nelson, Inc., P.O. Box 141000, Nashville, TN 37214.

W Publishing Group books may be purchased in bulk for educational, business, fundraising, or sales promotional use. For information, please email SpecialMarkets@ThomasNelson.com.

Published in association with Yates & Yates, LLP, Attorneys and Counselors, Orange, California.

Editorial Staff: Shady Oaks Studio, 1507 Shirley Way, Bedford, TX 76022
Cover Design: TOBIAS' OUTERWEAR FOR BOOKS

ISBN 1-4185-1411-X

Printed in the United States of America
06 07 08 09 VG 9 8 7 6 5 4 3 2

FROM THE BIBLE-TEACHING MINISTRY OF CHARLES R. SWINDOLL

Charles R. Swindoll has devoted his life to the clear, practical teaching and application of God's Word and His grace. A pastor at heart, Chuck has served as senior pastor to congregations in Texas, Massachusetts, and California. He currently pastors Stonebriar Community Church in Frisco, Texas, but Chuck's listening audience extends far beyond a local church body. As a leading program in Christian broadcasting, *Insight for Living* airs in major Christian radio markets around the world, reaching churched and unchurched people groups in language they can understand. Chuck's extensive writing ministry has also served the body of Christ worldwide, and his leadership as president and now chancellor of Dallas Theological Seminary has helped prepare and equip a new generation for ministry. Chuck and Cynthia, his partner in life and ministry, have four grown children and ten grandchildren.

Based on the original outlines, charts, and transcripts of Charles R. Swindoll's sermons, the workbook text was developed and written by Mark Gaither, Th.M., Dallas Theological Seminary, Dallas, Texas.

Contextual support material was provided by the Creative Ministries Department of Insight for Living.

Editor in Chief: Cynthia Swindoll, President, Insight for Living
Vice President: Wayne Stiles, Th.M., D. Min., Dallas Theological Seminary
Theological Editor: Michael J. Svigel, Th.M., Ph.D. candidate, Dallas Theological Seminary
Editor: Amy LaFuria Snedaker, B.A., English, Rhodes College

Active Spirituality

Bedside Blessings

Behold . . . The Man!

The Bride

Come Before Winter

Compassion: Showing We Care in a Careless World

The Darkness and the Dawn

David: A Man of Passion and Destiny

Day by Day

Dear Graduate

Dropping Your Guard

Elijah: A Man of Heroism and Humility

Encourage Me

Esther: A Woman of Strength and Dignity

Fascinating Stories of Forgotten Lives

Fascinating Stories of Forgotten Lives Workbook

The Finishing Touch

Five Meaningful Minutes a Day

Flying Closer to the Flame

For Those Who Hurt

Getting Through the Tough Stuff

Getting Through the Tough Stuff Workbook

God's Provision

The Grace Awakening

The Grace Awakening Devotional

The Grace Awakening Workbook

Great Attitudes!

Great Days with Great Lives

Growing Deep in the Christian Life

Growing Strong in the Seasons of Life

Growing Wise in Family Life

Hand Me Another Brick

Home: Where Life Makes Up Its Mind

Hope Again

Improving Your Serve

Intimacy with the Almighty

Job: A Man of Heroic Endurance

Job: Interactive Study Guide

Joseph: A Man of Integrity and Forgiveness

Killing Giants, Pulling Thorns

Laugh Again

Leadership: Influence That Inspires

Living Above the Level of Mediocrity

Living Beyond the Daily Grind, Books I and II

The Living Insights Study Bible, general editor

Living on the Ragged Edge

Living on the Ragged Edge Workbook

Make Up Your Mind

Man to Man

Marriage: From Surviving to Thriving

Marriage: From Surviving to Thriving Workbook

Moses: A Man of Selfless Dedication

The Mystery of God's Will

Paul: A Man of Grace and Grit

The Quest for Character

Recovery: When Healing Takes Time

The Road to Armageddon

Sanctity of Life

Shedding Light on Our Dark Side

Simple Faith

Simple Trust

So, You Want to Be Like Christ?

So, You Want to Be Like Christ? Workbook

Starting Over

Start Where You Are

Strengthening Your Grip

Stress Fractures

Strike the Original Match

The Strong Family

Contents

A Letter from Chuck

On June 18, 1955, Cynthia and I started a journey that has taken us through more than five decades (so far), countless miles, and experiences we never could have imagined in the beginning. At the tender ages of twenty and eighteen, we settled into a quiet, respectable routine in the little town of Channelview, Texas, where I was serving my apprenticeship to become a machinist. We worked hard, enjoyed each other's families, actively participated in church, and planned to start a family of our own, in a little house of our own. We had dreams for a great marriage.

As will occur in every life and in every marriage, we suffered a number of events that then felt like tragedies, painful circumstances that stressed our faith and strained our marriage. Some of those trials came from outside circumstances, but many came from within. And, I must confess, sometimes our marriage merely survived.

During some of those early, difficult years, we knew God wanted more for our marriage than basic survival, and *we* certainly wanted more. Instinctively, we knew that a good marriage would not happen automatically. After all, we were then as we are now: two sinful people in daily need of a Savior's enablement and each other's forgiveness. So, early on, we committed ourselves to keep Christ at the center of our marriage and to seek His mind in the pages of Scripture. We said to each other, "If it's written in His Word, then we will do whatever it says."

The workbook you are holding and its companion book, *Marriage: From Surviving to Thriving*, contain much of what Cynthia and I learned together. Every lesson comes straight from the pages of Scripture and reflects the insight of two people who sometimes had to learn the hard way. The principles contained in these two volumes are not merely good theory—what I *think* to be effective—but time-tested, tried-and-true methods for making your marriage everything God desires it to be and, therefore, the marriage you long to have.

I encourage you to take it slowly. Use the Bible lessons and carefully crafted questions to search your heart as you absorb and interact with God's Word. Before you begin, make this commitment to the Lord, to yourself, and to your mate: If it's written in His Word, then I will do whatever it says.

That's a bold promise. It will require all the trust you can gather. But I promise, if you follow through, your marriage will move from surviving to thriving.

Charles R. Swindoll

How to Use This Workbook

The goal of this workbook is simple: to provide you with encouragement, biblical principles, application, and practical insights that will help you discover what God intends for you and your mate to enjoy in marriage. Yes, He wants your marriage to last a lifetime, and He has so many delights waiting for you to experience today. This workbook can serve as a tool for personal devotions or as a guide to help couples interact with Scripture as it relates to marriage. Leader helps and a straightforward outline also make this an ideal resource for small group studies and church curriculum.

A brief introduction to its structure will help you get the most from your study.

 THE HEART OF THE MATTER highlights the main idea of the lesson and summarizes the corresponding chapter in the *Marriage: From Surviving to Thriving* hardcover book. The lesson itself is composed of three main teaching sections—"You Are Here," "Discovering the Way," and "Starting Your Journey." Take a moment to look through the first chapter of the workbook and become familiar with these three main sections found in every chapter.

 YOU ARE HERE includes an introduction and thought-provoking questions to orient you to the material covered in the chapter. Groups should plan to spend ten to fifteen minutes in this section.

DISCOVERING THE WAY explores the principles of Scripture through observation and interpretation of key passages, demonstrating the relevance of the Bible to modern life. Parallel passages and additional questions supplement the key Scriptures for more in-depth study. This section should require twenty to thirty minutes of group time.

 STARTING YOUR JOURNEY focuses on specific, activity-oriented applications to help you put into practice the principles of the lesson in ways that fit your personality, gifts, and level of spiritual maturity. A group should cover this section in about ten to fifteen minutes.

In the workbook's expanded margins, you'll find insightful quotations and helpful notes with suggestions for small-group study. If you're leading a time of group discussion, you'll find the Leader Helps to be invaluable in your preparation to teach each lesson.

USING THE WORKBOOK FOR SMALL-GROUP STUDY

Designed with the small group in mind, the *Marriage: From Surviving to Thriving Workbook* will be most effective when studied by two or more people with a facilitator. The following suggestions are recommended if you're serving as the small-group facilitator.

Preparation. All group members should try to prepare in advance during the week by working through the lessons as described later under "Using the Workbook for Individual Study or Couple Interaction." As the leader, you should take additional steps to supplement your preparation either by reading the corresponding chapter in the *Marriage: From Surviving to Thriving* hardcover book or listening to the corresponding sermon. Mastery of the material will build your confidence and competence, and approaching the topic from various perspectives will equip you to freely guide small-group discussion.

 Discussion Questions. You should feel free to mold the lesson according to the needs of your unique group. At a minimum, however, the group should cover the questions marked by the group icons in each of the three main sections during your time together. While planning the lesson you will want to mark additional questions you feel will fit the time allotment, needs, and interests of the group. The questions are divided to assist you in your lesson preparation. Note that the questions marked by the clock icon begin a series of *primary,* or core, questions—meant to contribute to a solid understanding of the lesson. The unmarked series of questions are *secondary*—intended to provide a deeper exploration of the topic and corresponding Scripture passages. Encourage your group to dig into the secondary questions on their own.

Flexibility. During group time, after opening in prayer, lead the group through the lesson you planned in advance. Members may want to share their own answers to the questions, contribute their insights, or steer the discussion in a particular direction that fits the needs of the group. Sometimes group members will want to discuss questions you may have left out of the planned lesson. *Be flexible,* but try to stay on schedule so the group has sufficient time for the final section, "Starting Your Journey," where the application of the lesson begins.

Goal. If it's unrealistic to complete a single lesson during a session, consider continuing where you left off in the next session. The goal is not merely to cover material, but to promote in-depth, personal discussion of the biblical text with a view toward personal response and application. To do this, the group will need to both understand the biblical principles and apply them to their lives.

USING THE WORKBOOK AS A COMPANION TO THE SERMON SERIES AND BOOK

For the greatest depth of study, this workbook should be used as a companion to the book by Charles R. Swindoll, *Marriage: From Surviving to Thriving* (Nashville, Tenn.: W Publishing Group, 2006). Each lesson in the workbook corresponds to the same chapter in the book. The workbook can also be used as a companion to Chuck's sermon series *Marriage: From Surviving to Thriving,* available from Insight for Living at www.insight.org.

USING THE WORKBOOK FOR INDIVIDUAL STUDY OR COUPLE INTERACTION

The *Marriage: From Surviving to Thriving Workbook* will facilitate your search through the Scriptures for what God has to say about marriage. Many of the questions are designed to be answered and shared by a couple in order to increase mutual understanding and encourage a common vision for how their partnership will grow. It can also be used for individual study. Here's the method we recommend.

Prayer. Begin each lesson with prayer, asking God to teach you through His Word and to open your heart to the self-discovery afforded by the questions and text of the workbook.

Any discipline must be approached with faith in God who alone can effect spiritual growth in our lives.

Scripture. Have your Bible handy. As you progress through each workbook chapter, you'll be prompted to read relevant sections of Scripture and answer questions related to the topic. You will also want to look up Scriptures noted in parentheses.

Questions. As you encounter the workbook questions, approach them wisely and creatively. Not every question will be applicable to each person all the time. If you can't answer a question, continue on in the lesson. Let the Holy Spirit guide you through the text and its application, using the questions as general guides in your thinking rather than rigid forms to complete.

Features. Throughout the chapters, you'll find several special features designed to add insight or depth to your study. Use these features to enhance your study and deepen your knowledge of Scripture, history, theology, and your mate. An explanation of each feature can be found on the next page.

As you complete each lesson, close in prayer, asking God to apply the wisdom and principles to your life by His Holy Spirit. Then trust that God will work out His will for you in His way, and that His Word will bear fruit.

Special Workbook Features

Lessons are supplemented with a variety of special features to summarize and clarify teaching points or to provide opportunities for more advanced study. Although they are not essential for understanding and applying the principles in the lesson, they will offer valuable nuggets of insight as you work through the material.

GETTING TO THE ROOT

While our English versions of the Scriptures are reliable, studying the original languages can often bring to light nuances of the text that are sometimes missed in translation. This feature explores the meaning of the underlying Hebrew or Greek words or phrases in a particular passage, sometimes providing parallel examples to illuminate the meaning of the inspired text.

DIGGING DEEPER

Various passages in Scripture touch on deeper theological questions or confront modern worldviews and philosophies that conflict with a biblical worldview. This feature will help you gain deeper insight into specific theological and practical issues related to the biblical text.

DOORWAY TO HISTORY

Sometimes the chronological gap separating us from the original author and readers clouds our understanding of a passage of Scripture. This feature will take you back in time to explore the surrounding history, culture, and customs of the biblical world as they relate to the text.

HEART TO HEART

This feature is specially designed to help couples interact with one another as they apply a primary principle from each lesson. They are practical and can be intense for some couples. They will take time and vulnerability, but the results are well worth the effort.

Our prayer is that the biblical principles and applications you glean from this resource will help you cultivate the kind of marriage that makes others wonder, *What's their secret?* May God's Word illumine the path before you and inspire you to deepen your intimacy with the Lord and with the mate He has given you for life.

Lesson One

This Is Not Your Grandfather's Family

— Selected Scriptures —

THE HEART OF THE MATTER

Today's family bears little resemblance to the family of the last generation. While the times and the families have changed, we can be sure that God's Word—the only reliable source of truth—will always remain the same. Following His Word will help our marriage not only survive but thrive. To prepare for this lesson, read Deuteronomy 6:5–12 and verse 24; then read chapter 1 in *Marriage: From Surviving to Thriving*.

YOU ARE HERE

Imagine you are a modern-day Rip van Winkle flipping on the tube as you settle down for an afternoon nap in 1966. Rob and Laura Petrie sleep in twin beds on *The Dick Van Dyke Show,* and NBC keeps Barbara Eden's navel discreetly covered on *I Dream of Jeannie.* While the Smothers Brothers have begun to push the edge of decency with some off-color content, the alternative, *Bonanza,* honors the values you want your children to emulate. Words like *abortion, incest, homosexuality,* and *condom* are never mentioned on television and certainly not from a pulpit or in schools.

As you drift off to sleep, you feel reasonably secure in a life that is good. It's not perfect, but it's simple, stable, predictable. You and your mate desire to create a safe, godly household, and your society is, for the most part, your ally. Then . . .

You open your eyes forty years later. Your culture has changed. It no longer supports your desire to maintain a God-centered home. Let's examine some of the challenges you face.

List the television programs produced in the last five years that portray the kind of family relationships you would like to have. What values do they represent that you find inspiring?

Think of your favorite television show involving a husband and wife or, if you don't watch much television, one you are most familiar with. In what ways do the characters reflect the traditional husband and wife roles?

Leader Help
Prepare a list of popular television programs that portray married couples. Ask group members which characters they most admire and which ones draw their greatest disapproval. Try to uncover the ways in which society influences how we think about marriage.

In what ways do they alter the traditional roles?

How do you think these changes would work in the real world?

Imagine you are chatting with a couple at church. During the conversation, you discover that they are not married and are living together. Describe your internal reaction.

If you were to discover further that they are members of the church and consider themselves committed Christians, how would that affect your reaction?

The images of domestic roles have become so smeared that we can barely recognize them. A masculine father who carries out his role as the spiritual leader of the family must do so apologetically. However tender and sensitive his approach, our culture will accuse him of being patriarchal and authoritarian. A feminine mother who delights in her role as caregiver and supporter will disappoint a watching world. Despite her dignified, sacrifical strength, too many will leave her with the odd feeling that she has something to prove.

—*Marriage: From Surviving to Thriving*

How do you think people of past generations would have responded? Would they be correct or incorrect?

 How much influence do you think the Bible has on shaping family life in your culture? Is the situation improving or getting worse? Why?

 ## DISCOVERING THE WAY

Through the decades as new families re-placed the older generations, the world obviously changed . . . and it's going to keep changing. Yet it's comforting to know that in the midst of the sometimes chaotic and cataclysmic societal upheavals, some things never change.

Search for Truth

Even as culture, technology, and family values seem to change with the wind, we need to focus our attention on a few unchanging truths.

First, *the heart of humanity hasn't changed.* You and I are by birth, nature, and choice depraved, that is, entirely corrupt. In our fallen condition, sin affects everything we think, say, and do (Jeremiah 17:9; Romans 3:10–12). Without the Holy Spirit, we could never halt our moral slide.

Second, *God's desire for His people hasn't changed.* God is holy, just, and pure, and He expects us to be holy as well (1 Peter 1:13–16). Though we could never do this in our own power, God grants us the power to fulfill what He commands by His Spirit.

Third, *God continues to be faithful and compassionate, and He wants us to be faithful and compassionate.* We can stand against what is clearly wrong and contrary to Scripture, while still showing grace and love toward those who live another way (Ephesians 4:15; 1 Peter 3:15).

Fourth, *God's truth remains unchanged, as revealed in the Scriptures.* As popular media challenge traditional concepts and desensitize our moral nerves, we can count on the Bible to reflect the unchanging mind of God, the source of all truth (John 17:17; 2 Timothy 3:16).

Hope for the Family in General and Your Marriage in Particular

The events described in the book of Deuteronomy took place after Israel had experienced several drastic changes. After centuries of slavery in Egypt, the Israelites had seen God bring down plagues, part the Red Sea, and lead them with pillars of cloud and fire. Within just a few months, their entire way of life had changed.

However, while camped on the edge of the Promised Land, the people failed to trust God in the face of superior armies and fortified cities. To punish the unbelieving generation, the Lord forced the Hebrews to live as nomads in the wilderness for forty years. Yet God continued to miraculously protect them and provide for their needs—both physical and spiritual.

At the time Moses wrote Deuteronomy, a new generation was standing on the threshold of the Promised Land—a blessing that would introduce a whole new set of challenges. Change always brings challenges. To pre-

Leader Help
Ask the group to share a short story of a major life change they experienced and how that affected their relationship with the Lord. The stories can be about an individual or about a couple, and the change may have had either a good or bad impact on their spiritual life.

pare the Israelites for what they were about to face, Moses reiterated the Law of God, beginning with the supreme commandment. The Jews call it the Shema, a passage they still consider to be the foundation of their faith.

GETTING TO THE ROOT

Jewish people call Deuteronomy 6:4–5 "the Shema" because the first word of verse 4 is the Hebrew word *shema*, "to hear." The verb is a command: "Listen!" Because it has other important nuances in Hebrew, such as "hearken," "understand," and "obey," this command conveys something beyond passively hearing the words. In William Shakespeare's *Julius Caesar*, Mark Antony cried, "Friends, Romans, countrymen, lend me your ears." In Deuteronomy, Moses demanded, "Israel, lend me your ears, your minds, your hearts, and your hands!"

Read Deuteronomy 6:4–12. This passage includes several orders after the command, "Listen!" Record them in the space below using short phrases.

You shall ___*love the Lord*___ (v. 5)

These words shall _____ (v. 6)

You shall _____ (v. 7)

and shall _____ (v. 7)

You shall _____ (v. 8)

and they shall _____ (v. 8)

You shall _____ (v. 9)

Then _____ (v. 12)

Our goal in this book is not to recover a bygone era, but to remain current and relevant without compromising our commitment to the truth of God's Word.

—*Marriage: From Surviving to Thriving*

According to verse 7, when were men and women supposed to discuss God's Word?

"Talk of them:
    when _____
        and _____
            and _____
               and _____."

The implications of this passage go further than memorizing a few verses, praying at mealtimes, and having family devotions. Describe how Scripture should function in the household.

Deuteronomy 6:24 explains why God wants His Word to permeate the home. What reason does it give?

DOORWAY TO HISTORY

For many centuries, devout Hebrews took the command of Deuteronomy 6:8–9 literally by attaching two small, leather boxes—one fastened to the forehead and one to the left hand—during morning prayers.

Inside each box, or *phylactery*, was a piece of parchment inscribed with the text of Deuteronomy 6:4–9, Deuteronomy 11:13–21, and God's name *Shaddai* (Almighty), to remind them of the Lord's constant presence and the importance of His Word.

Jewish homes also had a small, tube-shaped container attached to the right doorpost of the front entrance, which many would kiss upon entering and leaving. Tucked inside was a *mezuzah*, a scroll bearing the same passages of Scripture and the name Almighty. Even today, nearly every entrance in modern Israel, including homes, offices, and stores, has a mezuzah attached to the doorframe.

 In Deuteronomy 6:10–11, the Lord warned Israel about the danger of prosperity, telling them "watch yourself" in verse 12. Why would prosperity cause Israel to forget Him?

How does this danger appear in your culture today? Be specific.

How can you defend your home against this danger?

STARTING YOUR JOURNEY

During the Israelites' exodus from Egypt and their wilderness wanderings, Moses had led God's people, prayed for them, inspired and taught them like a parent would his or her children. Then, on the borders of a new land and a new life, Moses had to release the Hebrews to live on their own, much like a parent must do with a grown child.

As we face our own opportunities and challenges, we must heed the words of Moses. Prosperity and the tantalizing influence of our culture will do little to strengthen our marriages and our homes. On the other hand, worshiping the Lord and allowing His Word to permeate every aspect of our home life will cause our marriages to survive and thrive. This involves four specific actions that we must apply consistently, each and every day in the years to come.

1. *Wake up! Complacency blinds us to reality.*
Beware of the progressive dulling of your moral edge. Adversity and hardship have a way of keeping us more aware of ourselves and our values. When times are good, we are less likely to question our motives and our values, and we may not realize how far our culture has taken us from God's standards. We may even begin to tolerate changes in our marriage we once thought unthinkable.

2. *Listen up! Knowledge sets us free.*
Jesus said, "If you continue in My word, then you are truly disciples of Mine; and you will know the truth, and

In an ever-changing world, this remains permanent. As we feel the tug of gravity pulling us toward an inescapable moral slide, we can cling to this: Our relationship with the Lord is good and necessary for our survival, and the family is still the very best way to ensure the good and survival of future generations.

—*Marriage: From Surviving to Thriving*

the truth will make you free" (John 8:31–32). God is the source of all truth, and the only reliable means of knowing His truth is the Bible. For our good and for our survival in our drifting society, we must read and study God's Word on a regular basis—daily is best.

 ## HEART TO HEART

Your spiritual journey with your mate can be one of the most intense and rewarding experiences of your marriage—right up there with physical intimacy. But you may never have explored the spiritual dimension of your relationship for a variety of reasons. Perhaps you never saw it modeled in your home, or your expectations may be putting you off, or you may find that pride is standing in your way. Whatever the reason, we encourage you to lay it aside and follow a few simple steps. Incorporate this exercise into your life on a consistent basis.

1. Set aside no fewer than thirty minutes where you can be alone and undisturbed. (This may be the most difficult part of this new habit.)
2. Have one partner choose a book of the Bible. (Once you have read the entire book, the other partner should choose which book to read next.)
3. Have one partner read one full chapter of Scripture. Stop and talk as it seems natural to you. If you run out of time before you finish, mark your place and begin there the next time. If you complete the chapter with no discussion at all, relax. Close in prayer.
4. Allow the partner who did not read to pray on behalf of the couple.

Some key words to remember during this time include *freedom, relaxation, consistency, honesty,* and *faithfulness.* Enjoy this time. As the spiritual leader of the family, the husband should be in charge of making this happen, but in the interest of intimacy and growth together, each partner should share in reading and praying equally.

---

3. *Step up! Discernment prompts us to act courageously.*
Let's face it, the traditional roles of husband and wife are not popular these days and have been called everything from oppressive to barbarian. To be fair, many Christians in centuries past have twisted God's Word to suit their distorted motives, including oppressive male domination at times. However, a close examination of Scripture reveals that God's idea of a husband-wife relationship includes differing roles and responsibilities but equal standing before God. When we experience marriage as the Lord intends, both partners enjoy mutual dignity and a growing satisfaction.

When we tune out the distracting messages of our culture, focus on hearing God's Word, and experience the benefits, we will naturally feel more confident in the face of criticism from the outside.

4. *Look up! God loves us unconditionally.*
An inherent danger lurks in even the best books on marriage and family. They can leave you with the impression that success is your responsibility. "Do this, do that, and then your marriage will last," is their unwitting message. Without a doubt you have a stake in the quality of your union, and what you do and don't do will have an effect. However, the Lord wants your marriage to give you joy and bring Him glory, and He will supernaturally work to

When we can see things as God sees them, and as we survey the world with God's perspective, we find within ourselves a kind of God-prompted supernatural courage to take a stand, to be different. It takes wisdom to do that without appearing either pathetic or condemning. While we want our difference to be attractive, we will nonetheless experience rejection and ridicule. Still we must act.

—*Marriage: From Surviving to Thriving*

make it survive and thrive. Success is His responsibility, if only we will yield control of our marriage, our mate, and our selves to Him.

 Spending time in Scripture and prayer as a couple is very difficult, even for people in full-time Christian ministry. What do you think are some reasons for this? What is the primary challenge to your doing this? Be as honest as you can.

Leader Help
The group question is very penetrating and may be uncomfortable, especially this early in the study. To be sensitive to this, assure the members that no one is required to answer aloud regarding his or her own struggles, but steer the discussion toward struggles all couples face. If you are comfortable, you might offer an answer from your own experience. If group members have not completed the prayer exercise that follows, you may assign it for homework or allot several minutes of class time for its completion.

Use the space beneath each passage of Scripture to compose a short prayer inviting the Lord to work in your marriage and committing your marriage relationship to God's care and control.

Genesis 2:24

Mark 12:29–30

Philippians 1:6; 2:12–13

Hebrews 13:20–21

In this lesson, we discovered that our attitudes about family often differ from not only those of the last generation but those of the Bible as well. In this light, we must keep God and His Word at the center of our marriages and continually commit them to the Lord's care and control. Only then will we set our feet on the right foundation for our marriages not only to survive *but to thrive.*

Notes

Notes

Notes

Lesson Two

Getting Back on Target

— Genesis 2:21–25; 3:8–13 —

THE HEART OF THE MATTER

When Adam and Eve sinned (Genesis 3), it ruined the marital paradise of the Garden (Genesis 2), and humans today continue to struggle with the consequences. In order to enjoy true intimacy despite the effects of the Fall, we must recognize the Lord's original plan for marriage and acknowledge the ways we've missed the mark. As we take responsibility for how we've blown it in the past, we will begin taking steps to get back on target and offer new life and hope to our marriages. To prepare for this lesson, read Genesis 2:21–25; 3:8–13; then read chapter 2 in *Marriage: From Surviving to Thriving*.

YOU ARE HERE

Marriage is God's invention; He showed us what it looks like in the story of the creation of Adam and Eve. In God's plan, the man and woman leave their respective families, commit themselves to one another for life, become one in terms of direction and mutual support, and enjoy an exclusive knowledge of each other. But sin spoiled the simplicity of

Leader Help

By the end of this lesson, group members should understand the four essential elements of a healthy marriage and examine their unions accordingly. They should be able to define *intimacy*, recognize how their sinful natures undermine intimacy, and choose constructive responses to wrongdoing in order to build intimacy.

biblical marriage. We have all strayed from the path of true intimacy that God originally outlined. To enjoy marital intimacy despite the Fall, we must see the target clearly and determine where we have gone off course.

 How does the world define *intimacy* in the marriage relationship? (Try to keep your answer to twenty-five words or fewer.)

How is that definition similar to your definition of *intimacy* as a Christian?

Describe in your own words what the phrase "one flesh" means.

 ## DISCOVERING THE WAY

Moses's summary statement in Genesis 2:24–25 establishes four key elements that bind two people together into a permanent, intimate union—marriage as God intended.

Four Principles from the First Wedding

Severance

> *For this reason a man shall leave his father and his mother* . . . (Genesis 2:24)

The Hebrew word for "leave" is most often translated "abandon." This does not imply that we are to ignore our parents or show them disrespect. But we are to change our primary allegiance from our old home to our new home, from parents to spouse, and to look to the marriage for our primary support.

Dr. Frank Minirth explains *severance* in the following way:

> "Leaving and cleaving" may feel like a betrayal and carry with it a fair amount of guilt. "How can I turn my back on the people that birthed me, fed me, loved me, and protected me for so many years?" Fortunately, the truth of the Bible gives you permission to devote yourself entirely to your new family unit, guilt free. Failure to do this will eventually strain every relationship you have.[1]

Permanence

> . . . *and be joined to his wife.* (Genesis 2:24)

A good picture of being joined permanently is the special glue that carpenters use to fuse two pieces of wood together permanently. Once dried, the wood will splinter before the bond will break. Such permanence allows each partner to rest in the security of a relationship that will never let him or her down, even when he or she fails to be a good mate. Without this security, neither partner will feel safe enough to reveal his or her authentic self.

Leader Help

As you review these principles during group time, read Genesis 2:24–25 aloud or write it on the board while pointing out the principle derived from each section of Scripture.

I've seen just as many men who won't cut the apron strings as women whose hearts belong to Daddy. I've seen women with such a bond with Mom there's no room for anyone else and men who depend upon Dad's checkbook as much as their own. And unless both partners in a marriage can "leave" their old families behind, their marriage can't possibly move on to the next level.

—*Marriage: From Surviving to Thriving*

Without permanence, attempts at intimacy will always be strained and tentative.

Perhaps you are not married to your first spouse because your first marriage ended in divorce. Don't let that stop you from applying this principle to your current marriage. Begin where you are. After all, it's never too late to start doing what is right. Regardless of what may have occurred in the past, determine that your current marriage is permanent. God has joined you; let no one and nothing separate you.

Unity

. . . and they shall become one flesh. (Genesis 2:24)

In this verse, God did not have in mind a melding of two personalities to form one individual. He doesn't want two bodies sharing one brain, but two individuals living and working together with a common set of values and pursuing shared goals. Unity brings differences into harmony without compromising the uniqueness of either individual.

 GETTING TO THE ROOT

The Hebrew word translated "one" in Genesis 2:24 "stresses unity while recognizing diversity within that oneness."[2] A good example would be Exodus 26:6:

You shall make fifty clasps of gold, and join the curtains to one another with the clasps so that the tabernacle will be *a unit.* (emphasis added)

The literal Hebrew is "so that the tabernacle will be one."

Intimacy

> *And the man and his wife were both naked and were not ashamed.* (Genesis 2:25)

Ultimately, intimacy is what we desire. Intimacy is the grand prize for all of the effort we put into our marriages. However, intimacy, like all great rewards, involves great risk and demands immense trust. What is it exactly?

> ***Intimacy between two persons is the process of knowing and being known without limitation.***

 How do the definitions of *intimacy* you discussed in the "You Are Here" section align with the definition above? How are they similar? Different?

Intimacy—this is our target. Pure, uninhibited, unselfish, blissful union enjoyed by two people made for each other. No barriers. No issues. No awkwardness. No hang-ups. Just intimacy.

—*Marriage: From Surviving to Thriving*

Intimacy Lost: Three Changes Introduced by Sin

Sin spoiled the simplicity of biblical marriage. The intimacy that came so naturally in Genesis 2 became quite *un*natural after the events of Genesis 3. The result is a triple threat to intimacy: self-consciousness, isolation (or self-protection), and fear. All three can be found in Genesis 3:7–8, which describe the first moments after Adam and Eve committed the first sin.

Self-Consciousness

 Read Genesis 2:25 and Genesis 3:7. Adam and Eve certainly understood that they weren't wearing clothes before their sin. In what way did their perception change after their sin?

Leader Help

Have some fun with this question, but be sensitive to the fact that some will be uncomfortable even imagining this. At the end, make the correlation to the experience of being emotionally nude and how it affects our interaction with our spouses.

Suppose you were suddenly transported to a public place and you had no clothes on. Describe how you would feel.

Isolation (or Self-Protection)

 Genesis 3:7 tells us that Adam and Eve made loin coverings. Exactly how many people lived on the earth at this point in the story? From whom did they cover themselves? Why do you think they did this?

How do isolation and self-protection manifest themselves in your relationship with your spouse? In other words, what tactics have become your fig leaves?

What situation causes you to run for cover most often?

What keeps you from choosing a more constructive response?

Fear

 Genesis 3:8 says that when Adam and Eve heard God enter the garden, they "hid themselves from the presence of the LORD God." How is Adam and Eve's response to God different than before they sinned?

What were Adam and Eve afraid would happen?

What effect did fear have on Adam and Eve's relationship, according to Genesis 3:12–13?

Did Adam or Eve lie? Explain your answer.

What should Adam have said in response to God's direct question in verse 11?

What should Eve's reply have been?

We can never regain the innocence and the intimacy of Genesis 2. Yet, all is not lost. We can enjoy intimacy, but only as we respond to wrongdoing constructively.

—*Marriage: From Surviving to Thriving*

John Milton called the scene of Genesis 3 *Paradise Lost*. Indeed, the simple, natural way of life that God gave the first humans has been lost to the effects of sin. The Lord announced the consequences of sin in the form of "curses." Hebrew has no fewer than six words that English translators render as "curse," but the one used in Genesis 3 carries a subtle, yet important nuance. According to one lexicon, the Hebrew term *arar* means "to bind (with a spell), hem in with obstacles, render powerless to resist."[3] God cursed the ground from bearing fruit without toil, He cursed childbirth from delivery without pain, and by extension, everything else in the world would follow suit—including marital intimacy.

 ## STARTING YOUR JOURNEY

Adam and Eve started their life together enjoying complete, uninhibited, unselfish intimacy. Then sin introduced at least three destructive forces into their marriage: selfishness, isolation (or self-protection), and fear. When confronted with their sin, the two responded with half-truths and finger pointing.

From their example, we know what behavior to avoid. We must deal with reality constructively, confessing the truth of any situation and accepting responsibility. If intimacy is the process of knowing and being known without limitation, then it must begin with our faults.

In Genesis 3:9–13, the Lord confronted Adam and Eve with a series of questions. He is omniscient (all-knowing), so we know that He didn't ask out of ignorance. He came to the garden with His wrath wrapped in grace. Confronting the first sinners with their sin was an act of mercy.

When it comes to our relationships, we need to ask ourselves some questions too. Take a moment to think

Leader Help

Depending on the comfort level of your group, you may select appropriate questions from this section to discuss during class. If you do, encourage the group members to make this a time for *self-disclosure*, not spouse disclosure, even if the question involves the perspective or behavior of their mate. Group members should hold each other accountable to this practice.

through the following questions relating your marriage to the principles we've discussed. Use them to seriously and honestly evaluate your relationship with your spouse and what it might take for you to get on target with God's plan for your marriage. Then determine a time to discuss your thoughts with your mate.

Severance

What does it mean to you that "a man must leave his father and mother and be joined to his wife" (Genesis 2:24)? How have you applied this in your marriage?

Which of the following statements most accurately describes your experience?

❏ **My mate sometimes complains that I am "too close" to one or both of my parents.**

❏ **My mate occasionally appears to be threatened by my relationship with my parent(s).**

❏ **I feel more comfortable in my parents' house than my own.**

❏ **I often turn to my parents for emotional or financial support.**

❏ **When I am stressed, the first person I think to approach is someone other than my spouse.**

❏ **Sometimes I'm afraid I will hurt my parents' feelings by putting my spouse first.**

❏ **One or both of my parents complain or otherwise indicate that I have become distant or that they have "lost" me since the wedding, and I feel guilty.**

Unity

In the space below, list what you perceive to be your spouse's four top priorities in life and four core values. (A core value is a foundational "principle, standard, or quality considered worthwhile or desireable."[4])

PRIORITIES	VALUES
Healthy, happy children	Efficiency

Based on your list, in what ways do your own priorities and values conflict with those of your mate?

How have these conflicting values and priorities affected your relationship? How have you handled any conflicts? Be specific.

Permanence

I'm generally against divorce; however, I would consider it if:

❑ My spouse had an affair.

❑ My spouse became terminally ill or permanently debilitated.

❑ My spouse stopped loving me.

❑ We grew apart in terms of our direction in life.

❑ I fell madly in love with someone else.

❑ Our finances changed dramatically.

❑ One or all of our children died or moved away.

❑ Other:_____.

Intimacy

Intimacy requires us to be comfortable with self-disclosure. If you were to use clothing to describe your willingness to be known by your partner, how would you gauge your vulnerability? Give an example of how this affects your marriage.

❑ Suit of Armor

❑ Fire Suit

❑ Surgical Scrubs

❑ Fig Leaves

❑ Birthday Suit

Using the same scale, how would you gauge your partner's vulnerability?

Leader Help

Just for fun, paste pictures of the different clothing to a poster board and ask the group members to write their names under the pictures that best describe their vulnerability within the marriage.

Place a check next to the statements regarding intimacy that apply to your marriage.

❑ We hardly know each other.

❑ I have qualities that I am ashamed for my partner to see.

❑ Allowing my partner to see me nude makes me feel self-conscious.

❑ Some people in my life know things about me that my mate does not.

❑ I can tell my spouse anything.

❑ I feel comforted that my partner knows everything about me.

❑ I have a hard time admitting to my mate that I am wrong or have failed.

❑ I am a safe place for my mate to admit his or her faults and my mate knows this.

❑ I want my spouse to see a better person in me than I know I am.

❑ I try to help my partner see his or her faults so my partner can grow.

❑ I feel it's important to impress my partner, even after years of marriage.

❑ My mate accepts my body without criticism, even when I'm critical of myself.

❑ My spouse knows what I want for Christmas or birthdays.

❑ If money were no object, shopping for my partner would be very easy.

❑ I want to know more about my mate just because I enjoy knowing him or her better.

❑ I deliberately find something about myself to tell my partner that he or she didn't know.

❑ My mate and I enjoy each other's company because we can be ourselves.

❑ My mate frequently disappoints me with his or her behavior.

❑ My partner's values and priorities could use some improvement.

❑ My partner and I have discussed our values and priorities.

If you and your spouse were given free, confidential counseling to solve any marital problem, however large or small, what would you tell the counselor first?

Does the answer you just wrote involve the failings of your mate or your own?

The story of Adam and Eve tells us that intimacy is not beyond our reach. It can never be what it was before sin entered the scene, but it can be good. But like the ground, our marriages will only bear fruit "by the sweat of our faces."

Leader Help

The culmination of this lesson is the "Heart to Heart" exercise. Encourage the members to recognize that, because "all have sinned" (Romans 3:23), the need for confession and repentance to our mates is not optional. Each member should leave the session with plans to approach his or her spouse with an apology without delay.

 ## HEART TO HEART

Getting your marriage back on target doesn't involve fixing your mate. Step back and allow the Holy Spirit to do that. Instead, try to determine what you have done or are doing that contributes to what you see as a problem. A good place to begin would be your answer to the "counselor" question above or any issues that may have surfaced in the "Starting Your Journey" section. Take a moment to acknowledge your own shortcomings before God and ask for His help. Then follow the very difficult path outlined below. It's risky. It requires self-disclosure and the possibility of being hurt. But this is the surest way to build intimacy between two imperfect people.

Begin by pinpointing some specific way you have offended or disappointed your mate. Choose something manageable yet significant to your mate. Jot it down in the margin or use a separate sheet of paper (you may wish to take notes or write down your thoughts along the way). Now move through the following steps:

Stop. Accept the truth of your poor choices or outright sin, and own the responsibility for the damage your action or inaction has caused.

Repent. Confess your failure to the Lord in prayer, and commit yourself to turning from it. Ask Him for His help. He has promised to provide you with the strength to meet this challenge.

Confess. Tell your mate how you have failed or have contributed to making a situation worse. Be careful not to include any mention of his or her wrongdoing, and resist the temptation to minimize yours.

Restore. Apologize, showing genuine concern for how you have hurt your mate or the marriage. Your sorrow should reflect the level of your mate's pain.

Rest. Receive the Lord's forgiveness, and accept that your mate may or may not respond as you might want.

Review. Without being too hard on yourself, try to discover why you chose to act as you did. Choices arise from expectations—usually subconscious ones. Ask the Lord to show you what you don't see so that you can replace destructive coping with constructive choices.

With each question, the Lord gave Adam, then Eve, an opportunity to come clean with the whole truth, repent, and ask forgiveness. But with each question, the man and woman failed to respond as they should.

—*Marriage: From Surviving to Thriving*

Once you have successfully addressed one issue, choose another, then another. Make this a habitual part of your relationship. Before long, you'll find that the difficulties that complicate your marriage are shrinking as you move closer together. You'll also discover that the intimacy you gained was worth the risk.

☞

In this lesson, we discovered the essentials of intimacy as God intended—as well as several obstacles. Only by taking personal responsibility for our sin can we hope to enjoy true intimacy with our mates. What will you do this week to get your marriage back on target?

Notes

Notes

Notes

Lesson Three

Symphony of Survival in the Key of "C"

— Selected Scriptures —

THE HEART OF THE MATTER

Commitment is nothing more complicated than deciding to stay with your partner, no matter what. And commitment is the first priority in marriage. No amount of counseling, Bible study, or encouragement will help a marriage in which the partners are not seriously committed to staying together. When partners are committed to one another, a marriage can survive extreme challenges such as the consequences of sin, conflict between the partners, or difficult life circumstances. To prepare for this lesson, read Genesis 3:16–24; Hosea 1:2–9, 3:1–3; Matthew 1:18–21; then read chapter 3 in *Marriage: From Surviving to Thriving*.

YOU ARE HERE

Very often, men and women fall in love and decide that marriage is the next logical step, perhaps expecting that it will encourage greater intimacy or "complete" the relationship. Soon, however, they discover that the marriage covenant doesn't make intimacy any easier. When the storms of life beat down on their union, the option to

Leader Help
By the end of this lesson, group members should recognize that commitment is a biblical mandate for marriage, a decision that requires faith, and one that can transcend all challenges. They should also honestly evaluate their level of commitment and give tangible expression of their devotion to their mates.

Leader Help
The questions in this section may probe very tender areas for some group members. They may be experiencing a crisis that they have not discussed with others or with their mates. It's best to prepare ahead of time by asking one of the more experienced couples if they would be willing to supply answers to the group questions.

Commitment is a biblical mandate for marriage. And like all biblical mandates, it requires faith to see beyond the immediate and offers unseen rewards when obeyed. Take it from a guy who's been married for fifty years: that one-flesh union won't maintain itself, but it's worth the effort.
—*Marriage: From Surviving to Thriving*

escape can appear very attractive. Disillusionment can be overwhelming. Many find themselves saying, "I thought things would be better after we married, but . . . "

Describe your expectations coming into marriage. What did you expect your relationship or your life together to be like?

What was your first indication that some of your expectations might never be realized? How did you respond?

How did this affect your view of your mate?

Almost every married person has faced or will face a crisis—a challenge or disappointment so great that he or she questions the decision to marry or to stay in the marriage.

Is this your experience now?
☐ Yes   ☐ No

If this is your experience now, what do you feel must happen to keep the marriage from falling apart?

Have you and your mate faced a crisis at some time in the past?

☐ Yes   ☐ No

If you have experienced this before, what kept you and your mate together?

How did your thinking about marriage, your mate, and yourself change after having persevered through that crisis of commitment?

> If marriage is going to survive, commitment is "priority one." Very little else you do in a marriage will matter if you haven't determined to stay in it.
>
> —*Marriage: From Surviving to Thriving*

DISCOVERING THE WAY

A significant milestone for many couples is the realization that marriage is not the final destination of their romance but the beginning of a promise. When they surrender their magical view of marriage and accept that the world didn't change after the wedding, the meaning of their vows sinks in, perhaps for the first time: *commitment*. "For better or for worse, for richer or for poorer, in sickness and in health, until death parts us." Those vows honor the words of Jesus. When asked about marriage, He said, "So they are no longer two, but one flesh. Therefore what God has joined together, let no man separate" (Matthew 19:6).

Three couples in the Bible adequately demonstrate that a marriage can survive virtually any challenge, as long as the people remain committed to one another.

The Challenge of Consequences (Adam and Eve)

 The verses in the left column describe the life and purpose of Adam and Eve before they sinned. In the right column, describe how life changed as a result of sin. We have included a verse reference to guide you as well as an example.

Before the Fall	Result of the Fall
God blessed them; and God said to them, "Be fruitful and multiply, and fill the earth, and subdue it." (Genesis 1:28)	Genesis 3:16a *The woman will endure great pain during childbirth. Reproduction now involves great sorrow.*
Then God said, "Behold, I have given you every plant yielding seed that is on the surface of all the earth, and every tree which has fruit yielding seed; it shall be food for you." (Genesis 1:29)	Genesis 3:17b–18:
The man said, "This is now bone of my bones and flesh of my flesh." (Genesis 2:23)	(NOTE: See "Getting to the Root" on the following page.) Genesis 3:16b:

Then the LORD God took the man and put him into the garden of Eden to cultivate it and keep it. (Genesis 2:15)	Genesis 3:23–24
And the man and his wife were both naked and were not ashamed. (Genesis 2:25)	Genesis 3:7, 21
God saw all that He had made, and behold, it was very good. (Genesis 1:31)	Romans 8:20–22

GETTING TO THE ROOT

Genesis 3:16 presents an interesting challenge for interpreters. The Hebrew reads, literally, "toward your husband, your desire." Sometimes ancient languages will omit the main verb in one sentence, intending to borrow the meaning from an adjacent sentence. In this case, the sentence "toward your husband, your desire" reaches forward to borrow "to rule," from "and he will rule over you."

Genesis 4:7 uses the same type of expression when referring to the relationship between Cain and sin: "Toward you, its desire," followed by the clause, "you must rule over it."

Because each curse that God pronounced added enmity and difficulty to each relationship (between the woman and the serpent, the serpent and her "seed," the man and the ground, etc.), we should expect the same between the man and the woman. She would desire to rule over him, but he would dominate her. The curse predicts that husbands and wives would, thanks to the polluting effects of sin, no longer enjoy a relationship completely free of power struggles.

If anyone struggled with the effects of sin on a marriage, Adam and Eve did. Yet we have no reason to believe that they ever ceased to live as husband and wife. Their example tells us that a marriage can survive the harsh consequences of poor choices and even outright sin.

The Challenge of Conflict (Hosea and Gomer)

 According to Hosea 1:2, what kind of woman did the Lord instruct Hosea to marry?

The phrase "wife of harlotry" most likely refers to what Gomer would become rather than what she was at the time of the wedding. After bearing three children, two of whom Hosea may not have fathered, Gomer abandoned the family for a life of prostitution. An unknown period of time passed—most likely years—during which Gomer apparently became so destitute that she sold herself into slavery.

According to Hosea 3:1, what difficult command did the Lord give Hosea?

If you were in Hosea's position, how difficult would this be for you, and what would be your greatest hindrance to obeying the command?

If Hosea had been living in New Testament times, what would his options have been according to Matthew 19:8–9?

Hosea obeyed the Lord. Describe his attitude as you see it in Hosea 3:2–3.

According to Leviticus 20:10, what did Gomer deserve?

Divorce will not erase the pain and the damage infidelity has done to your spirit. You must heal either way. The question is: how and with whom will you heal?

—*Marriage: From Surviving to Thriving*

Hosea's treatment of his unfaithful wife demonstrated extraordinary grace. Very few of us would be pushed to such an extreme. Hosea's case was special because of his duties as God's prophet. However, every marriage involves two sinners. Sin on a significant scale is quite likely. The example of Hosea and Gomer tells us that a marriage can endure the most severe conflict between the couple.

The Challenge of Circumstances (Joseph and Mary)

Sometimes difficulties in a marriage come not from the sinful natures of the couple or any conflict between them, but as a result of outside circumstances. Financial difficulties, struggles with the extended family or community, illness, death, natural disasters, or any unusual state of affairs can put a terrible strain on a relationship. The unrelenting stress can leave both husband and wife drained of the emotional strength required to maintain a healthy intimacy.

Consider the unusual set of circumstances that surrounded the betrothal and married life of Joseph and Mary: the messages from angels, the miraculous conception, the rumors, the wrath of Herod. Yet they stayed committed to each other through it all.

DOORWAY TO HISTORY

The marriage traditions that Joseph and Mary followed were quite different from those of our twenty-first-century Western culture. In the ancient Near East, the groom's parents usually sought out a suitable mate for their son and negotiated a marriage contract with the bride's parents. The young couple may or may not have been consulted, but in most cases, their desires were taken into account.

Once an agreement was reached, the parents sealed a contract at the local synagogue and made arrangements for the ceremony, which often took place a year or more later. During this "betrothal" period, the man and the woman were considered a married couple in the eyes of God and the community, although they were not to consummate the union with physical intimacy until after the ceremony. Before the ceremony, sexual relations by either party were considered adultery, not just fornication (see Deuteronomy 22:23–24).

Mary's condition during the betrothal period gave the community ample reason to suspect the worst. Either she and Joseph had been intimate or Joseph was marrying a defiled woman, a choice that would have defiled him in the eyes of the religious leaders.

Matthew 1:18–25 describes a wonderful, yet highly unusual, event in the lives of Joseph and Mary. They knew the truth of their unusual pregnancy, but no one else in their community received similar visits by heavenly messengers. Read the passage and use your imagination in response to the following questions.

Read Matthew 1:18–25. If you were in Joseph and Mary's situation, how would you respond to the accusations of the community?

How would this affect your relationship with your spouse?

Joseph and Mary would have to rest confidently in the truth of their innocence and find contentment in that. No one would believe the truth no matter how hard they tried to convince them. Whispers and snickering and jokes and scorn would be their closest and most enduring companions. This would either draw them together, or it would become a wedge. They would either seek opposite corners of the house or turn toward each other for strength. Everything hinged on their commitment to each other.

—*Marriage: From Surviving to Thriving*

In what ways could Joseph and Mary allow their difficult circumstances to deepen their intimacy?

Both Joseph and Mary understood the difficulties associated with their decision to stick to their marriage commitment. They knew their obedience to God would cost them any hope of a normal marriage. The example of this wonderful pair reminds us that a marriage can endure the most difficult of circumstances when the couple commits to facing them together.

Leader Help

Encourage the couples to work through these questions beforehand, and then ask only couples who have discussed them to answer in the group. None of the answers should be a revelation to one of the partners. No partner should be put in a position to exclaim suddenly, "I didn't know that!"

STARTING YOUR JOURNEY

A marriage played in the key of "C" (commitment) can withstand the challenges of consequences, conflict, or circumstances. True commitment doesn't change with shifting fortunes of life, or with the ebb and flow of feelings, or even with poor behavior of either partner. Commitment is a promise made once for all time and then confirmed by the daily decision to stay rather than leave.

What do you think presents the greatest challenge to your marriage right now?

Suppose a messenger from heaven were to tell you that your spouse will never leave you under any circumstances and will continue to love you no matter what. How would that knowledge affect your response to the challenges you face?

What keeps you from giving this gift of assurance to your spouse today?

What behavior or habits do you have that would cause your spouse to doubt your promise of lifetime commitment? (You may have to ask your mate to answer this for you.)

What new behavior or habit can you develop that will reassure your spouse that your promise is reliable?

HEART TO HEART

The benefit of saying "I love you" as a natural part of your conversations with your mate should be obvious. But have you considered the value of repeating your vows to each other?

Your relationship will undoubtedly experience difficulties. Misunderstandings, callous comments, angry words, and countless other transgressions require regular repentance, confession, and forgiveness. Over time, however, these little offenses can chip away at the confidence you have in each other's commitment. Recalling for your mate the promises you spoke during the ceremony can be a wonderful way to encourage him or her during difficult times.

Take some time to purchase a box of cards and envelopes (or make cards using paper or index cards). This week, address one of them to your partner and write a love note using one of the promises you spoke during the ceremony. For instance, if you originally recited the traditional vows at your wedding, you might write something like this:

My Treasured Mate,

_____ (Number) years ago, I promised that I would remain committed to you "in prosperity and in want." I know that lately we have been having a difficult time with our finances, but I want you to know how happy I am that we are together, and I will be yours no matter what.

I love you,

_____

(your name)

Place the card in an envelope and put it where your mate will find it sometime during the week. Over a period of weeks, prepare new "promise reminders," each focusing on a different portion of your wedding vows. This can be a powerful intimacy builder, especially when the marriage is under stress.

Commitment is a simple concept that's anything but easy. Our selfish natures would have us believe that escape will ease our discomfort, that our problems are better faced alone than together. Even thousands of years after Adam and Eve retreated from each other in the garden, our urge to sew fig leaves is as strong as ever.

Because commitment is a matter of faith, we should not be surprised that it involves all the elements of faith: obvious risk, unseen reward, and a call to walk not by sight. Recall the commitment you first made, repeat it in your prayers, and then reassure your mate with tangible expressions of your resolve to stay, "no matter what."

I've never seen one marriage get worse when the partners redouble their commitment to one another. The problems may not go away, but the marriage only gets stronger.

—*Marriage: From Surviving to Thriving*

Notes

Notes

Notes

Lesson Four

Practical Advice on Making a Marriage Stick

— Ephesians 4:25–32 —

THE HEART OF THE MATTER

Paul wrote Ephesians 4:25–32 to the members of the church at Ephesus, giving them practical principles to apply in order to build unity. Five principles found among eleven commands give concrete expression to the quality of grace, which always draws people closer together. If the instructions in this passage can unify a church body, how much more will they sweeten a marriage? To prepare for this lesson, read Ephesians 4:25–32; then read chapter 4 in *Marriage: From Surviving to Thriving*.

YOU ARE HERE

Commitment may give a marriage longevity, but it doesn't guarantee that the time will be sweet. One couple may describe their many years together as unfulfilling, disappointing years, while another would call theirs comforting and satisfying.

Leader Help
By the end of this lesson, group members should appreciate the value of a grace-based marriage relationship, which involves no fewer than five principles that build upon commitment and, when practiced, allow two people to enjoy unity.

Leader Help

Encourage husbands and wives to work on this lesson separately and then to compare notes before the group meets. Establish a ground rule that couples should share answers in the group only when both feel comfortable doing so.

 How would you gauge the emotional climate of your marriage? Place an X along the line to indicate your assessment.

Hostile   Difficult   Detached   Satisfying   Blissful

◄――――――――――――――――――――――――――►

Without singling out either partner, explain why you rated this aspect of your marriage this way.

Compare notes with your partner, if possible, and indicate his or her assessment on your gauge with an O. What similarities and differences do you see in your descriptions?

How would you describe the emotional climate of the home in which you grew up? Place an X on the line for your answer; then place an O to indicate your mate's response.

Hostile   Difficult   Detached   Satisfying   Blissful

◄――――――――――――――――――――――――――►

How similar is the emotional climate of your marriage to that of your childhood home?

DISCOVERING THE WAY

Obviously, *love* is important to marriage, but how much thought have you given to *grace*? What does grace look like when expressed between people, specifically between husband and wife? Ephesians 4:25–32 was written to members of a church and offers no fewer than five principles that give practical expression to the idea of grace in relationships. Let's take a look at each principle and then discuss how to put them into practice. As you do, the result will most certainly be greater unity in your marriage and greater peace in your household.

FIVE PRINCIPLES THAT MAKE A MARRIAGE STICK

Cultivate Complete Honesty (Ephesians 4:25)

Complete the diagram below based on Ephesians 4:25:

"Therefore, laying aside falsehood, speak truth each one of you with his neighbor, for we are members of one another" (Ephesians 4:25).

The command: _____

Who is to do this: _____

To whom: _____

How: _____

Why: _____

What is the relationship between falsehood, trust, and intimacy, according to this verse?

Lying has many variations. It ranges from mild to extreme deception: diplomatic hedging, stretching the facts, not telling the whole story, staying silent when we should speak, whitewashing motives, flattery, twisting the truth, adding false details, making up facts, contriving stories, embracing fiction as truth. Lying doesn't fix things; it has the power to destroy intimacy in marriages.

—*Marriage: From Surviving to Thriving*

If you have hidden from your mate behind a veil of deception or a veneer of pretense, the first step of truth telling will be difficult. Self-disclosure is hard enough without having to confess falsehood, but truth and trust are necessary for intimacy.

Express Anger in Appropriate Ways and at the Right Time (Ephesians 4:26–27)

What is the first command in Ephesians 4:26?

What two conditions does Paul put on this command?

What does verse 27 suggest will be the consequences of anger that either leads to sin or persists without resolution?

How have you seen this scenario play out in your own life?

A marriage characterized by mutual respect will allow each partner enough room to express angry feelings.

—*Marriage: From Surviving to Thriving*

GETTING TO THE ROOT

"And do not give the devil an opportunity."
EPHESIANS 4:27

The word translated "opportunity" in Ephesians 4:27 is the Greek word *topos*, which simply means "place." Figuratively, this term can mean opportunity, sanctuary, or territory. The Old Testament often uses the word *place* to refer to a special location used to worship a god. In the New Testament, *topos* can refer to an official's position of authority in government or in the church. Paul probably brought all of these nuances to bear on his warning so that the verse could be paraphrased: "Do not erect a shrine to your anger in your heart. The devil will appoint himself its priest."

Expressing anger may seem counterproductive to enjoying a peaceful marriage, but the command is clear. Address sources of anger without delay, being careful to choose appropriate timing, and express anger in constructive rather than destructive ways.

Don't Steal from Your Mate (Ephesians 4:28)

 According to Ephesians 4:28, what is the mandatory alternative to stealing?

How does someone who either takes what rightfully belongs to another or takes more than his or her share harm the community?

What kind of "stealing" might affect intimacy in a marriage?

To foster greater intimacy, seek to contribute more to the marriage than you take out of it. When one person takes advantage of another, resentment and emotional distance are inevitable.

Closely Guard Your Speech (Ephesians 4:29–30)

 Ephesians 4:29 strictly prohibits what kind of speech? What is the only kind of speech permitted?

List some examples of each.

What form does "unwholesome" talk tend to take in your life?

What does verse 30 provide as a motivation for our following these commands?

James 3:1–12 leaves little doubt that the single most powerful weapon of evil and the most helpful instrument of good is the tongue. The emotional impact of ten good deeds can be wiped out by a single, accurately placed insult. On the other hand, the affirmation of a genuine compliment can inspire someone to become more than he or she was before.

Dale Carnegie, in his classic manual on effective management, *How to Win Friends and Influence People*, lists these as his first two rules in handling people: "Don't criticize, condemn or complain" and "Give honest and sincere appreciation."[1] These are good rules for any context, and they are especially well suited for marriage.

Be Nice (Ephesians 4:31–32)

 List the six destructive forces that Paul says must be driven out of the community (Ephesians 4:31).

What three behaviors are commended according to verse 32?

What is the significance of "just as" in verse 32?

"Nice" is a characteristic that we tend to withhold from those closest to us and to lavish on complete strangers in the general public. Yet who deserves our best behavior more than our spouse?

 Without turning the page, can you remember the five principles of grace from Ephesians 4:25–32? Write them below.

1.

2.

3.

4.

5.

STARTING YOUR JOURNEY

Observe couples who enjoy an easy tranquility and who genuinely like each other, and you will undoubtedly see the principles of Ephesians 4:25–32 at work. Such couples defy falsehood by choosing to remain vulnerable. Even if the truth makes them look bad, they trust their partner to accept them. Because they guard their words, they can be truthful in relative safety. They address offenses quickly and constructively, being careful to hear each other clearly. They honor one another by setting aside selfishness and seeking to meet the need of the other, sometimes at great cost.

These principles may come more naturally to some couples than to others. At the beginning of this study, you gauged the emotional climate of your childhood home. You may or may not have noticed a correlation between your upbringing and your marriage. The goal of the question is not to lay blame on anyone but to acknowledge that the principles presented in this chapter will come less naturally if they were not modeled for us. Regardless, we must set aside the expectation that these five principles will come effortlessly and be willing to "go to school" on them—to study and practice them like we would any skill.

Fortunately, you have a study partner (your spouse) and an excellent textbook (God's Word). Learning how to extend grace to each other can be a great way to begin your marriage, even if the wedding took place decades ago. Here's how.

Answer the following questions and have your spouse do the same. Then set aside some time to be alone with your spouse when you can talk at length without interruption. Read and explain your answers to one another as you progress through the steps.

Fifty years following our wedding, my goal now is to have a reasonably good marriage. I don't expect honeymoon bliss, although we enjoy times that come close. And I won't settle for a perpetual ceasefire, though sometimes that's the best we can do as we get past a disagreement.

—Marriage: From Surviving to Thriving

Step 1: Agree to set aside all disagreements and any desire to determine who is responsible for what, and commit yourselves to learning new skills.

Which is more important to you: enjoying a peaceful and fulfilling future, or being vindicated of any wrongdoing in the past? Answer carefully.

Step 2: Determine which of the five principles of Ephesians 4:25–32 comes least naturally to you.

Which of the principles do you most struggle to apply consistently?

Leader Help

Because this section will take extended time and effort, you might consider assigning this as homework for the next meeting time. If group members prepared ahead of time, the lesson will have either clarified some issues or given the group members a greater sense of urgency. Ask members to share what they gained from the exercise.

Which of the five principles were modeled poorly in your childhood home? Limit your answer to no more than two.

What would it take to reverse this trend in your current home?

Step 3: Confess your weakness to your partner and enlist his or her help. (Be honest about your needs. You'll have a chance to tell your spouse how he or she can help in step 4.)

How do you think your partner will react to your disclosure? Does this cause you anxiety?

If this causes you anxiety, what do you fear will happen?

In honor of "cultivating complete honesty," you might consider including your answers as you discuss step 3 with your mate. However, be careful to express them as *your* fear and not your mate's responsibility.

Step 4: Commit yourself to helping your partner with his or her weakness using encouragement only—positive words, affection, and praise—while avoiding all criticism and negative comments. (Even if your partner has not undertaken this study with you, you can resolve to support your partner anyway.)

What did your spouse list as his or her weakness?

 How, specifically, can you give positive encouragement to your spouse as he or she tries to improve? Feel free to ask your spouse for guidance.

Leader Help
This question may be helpful for group members to share; however, you might remind them to honor the privacy of their spouse as they respond.

Step 5: Look for opportunities to put the principle into action. The Heart to Heart exercise will help you get started.

Fellowship is built on trust, and trust is built on truth. So falsehood undermines fellowship, while truth strengthens it.

—JOHN R. W. STOTT[2]

HEART TO HEART

Learning to apply the grace principle you find least natural will not be easy. So you will need the help of your partner as you take your first, faltering step. Each principle listed below has an associated exercise. Remember, you are learning a new skill, which will take time, involve mistakes, and require patience for both partners. Approach these principles with cooperation in mind.

Choose one of the following action steps as you begin to apply the principles of grace-based relationships to your marriage.

☐ 1. *Cultivate Complete Honesty*

Choose one of the following facts about yourself: your greatest fear, an incident in your past in which you behaved poorly, or an unattractive quality that you know you have. This should be something about which your partner has little or no knowledge.

Sit with your partner so that you can see his or her eyes and hold both hands.

Begin with the words, "I am taking a risk in telling you this—not because of you, but because of my own fear."

Reveal your "secret" in one short sentence, and then allow your mate to absorb the information in silence. Resist the urge either to speak or to move from where you are.

The listening partner should temper any initial response. Your role is to be a safe place for your spouse to reveal anything. Respond only with the words, "Thank you for telling me this. I love you."

When both of you feel ready, share the details of your "secret" without justifying, minimizing, or defending.

Conclude your time by affirming your commitment to each other and saying a brief prayer of thanksgiving.

☐ *2. Express Anger in Appropriate Ways and at the Right Time*

For most people, responding to anger inappropriately is the result of having poor communication skills. For others, anger has much deeper roots. This issue is the topic of many excellent books, and any attempt to address it in so short a space could be more damaging than helpful. Therefore, we recommend the following resources if you find this principle particularly difficult to master:

> Chapman, Gary D. *The Other Side of Love: Handling Anger in a Godly Way.* Chicago: Moody, 1999.

> Carter, Les and Minirth, Frank. *The Anger Workbook.* Nashville: Thomas Nelson, 1993.

☐ *3. Don't Steal from Your Mate*

Stealing doesn't have to involve money or objects. We owe our mate our time, our affection, our trust, our confidentiality, our kindness, and more . . . the list could be endless. Perhaps it's time to exert some effort in giving rather than taking.

Begin with the following admission to yourself:

I am withholding _____
from my mate because _____
_____.

The reason may be either conscious or subconscious on your part.

Ask your partner this question: "As it relates to our marriage, do you feel cheated out of anything specific?" This question may require some explanation. Without leading your mate toward an answer, give

A marriage involves more than material possessions. It's a community of two, each having exchanged promises and expectations. My time, my trust, my work, my best self, even my body belongs in part to Cynthia. When I withhold or violate any of those things, I rob Cynthia of what is rightfully hers.

—*Marriage: From Surviving to Thriving*

an example, such as "time," "attention," or "affection." Your partner may need some time to reflect. Give him or her permission to tell you later, and then follow up in a day or so.

If your spouse cannot think of anything, don't give up. He may not know what he is missing! And she can't see your heart; only God can. Continue to pray about it, asking God to confirm or release your suspicions. If, on the other hand, your mate names something that you did not anticipate, humbly accept it and choose to work on giving in that area.

Giving your spouse what you have been withholding will undoubtedly require sacrifice. Loving this way is something we can't do in our own strength. Ask for God's help in keeping pride at bay and to soften your heart. Then choose what you will deny yourself in order to give to your mate and make the appropriate adjustments. It may also require creativity beyond your ability. Ask a trusted friend of the same gender as yourself for help. It may also require skills you don't possess. Confess this to your mate and ask for his or her help. Even if your first attempts are clumsy, your partner will appreciate the effort.

☐ 4. *Closely Guard Your Speech*

Negative comments and subtle criticisms come very naturally to our sinful nature. Positive speech—affirmation, compliments, encouragement—requires planning and deliberate action.

On a sheet of paper, begin a list of your partner's good qualities, such as talent, physical attractiveness, intelligence, resourcefulness—anything, great or small, that you see. List anything he or she does or has done for which you are thankful. This may be difficult, not because your mate has so little that's positive, but because you are not in the habit of noticing. Observation is a skill you will need to develop.

Choose one item from the list and communicate it in a positive way to your mate. Either write a short, two-sentence note; or better yet, say it directly. You might say, "I don't tell you this often enough, but _____."

Work toward communicating something positive in this way no less than twice each day. Keep the list going if you need to. In time, you will find more positive words to say on the spot. Don't save them. Say them as soon as they come to mind.

☐ 5. *Be nice*

The quality Paul has in mind in Ephesians 4:32 is gentleness. One way to express gentleness is by offering your mate a steady stream of small kindnesses. While the possibilities are limitless, the kind deeds that your mate will appreciate will be unique to him or her. Some examples would include:

For Her

Warm her car on a cold day.

Open doors for her.

Do a chore she normally does.

Give her an evening to be alone.

Ask what you can do to help her.

Learn how she takes her coffee or tea and prepare it for her.

Leave her nothing to carry but her purse

Just listen without giving advice.

For Him

Send him a love note or e-mail.

Give him time to unwind when he comes home.

Encourage him to have a night with the guys.

Thank him for being a good leader and provider.

Praise him in public.

Trust his judgment.

Plan a surprise date for him.

In other words, discover those small kindnesses that make your partner feel valued, and then incorporate them into your daily routine.

⚭

My authority on the subject of marriage doesn't come from fifty-plus years of doing marriage right. My authority comes from Scripture alone. We apply its principles, and we enjoy the benefits of obedience, but we also enjoy the grace of Christ, who keeps us going through the times we fail to practice what we know to be right.

—*Marriage: From Surviving to Thriving*

⚭

We encourage you to make these five steps of grace giving more than an exercise in a workbook. Make this the start of something permanent. Think of the principle you have chosen as a life skill that will enhance your marriage and, more importantly, the life of your mate. But don't expect this to become a natural part of you overnight. Work hard at cultivating these principles of grace, and you'll have a winning marriage that not only survives but thrives.

Notes

Notes

Notes

Lesson Five

Essential Glue for Every Couple to Apply

— 1 Corinthians 13:1–8 —

THE HEART OF THE MATTER

Love is a universal language, but it has a number of dialects. The Greeks called the passionate desire between men and women *eros*. They called the noble, companionate affection of one friend for another *phileo*. While both of these are a delightful part of a good marriage, neither will bond the couple like the kind of love called *agape*. Paul's grand treatise on *agape* in 1 Corinthians 13 describes this unique kind of love in practical terms that will help us determine whether or not we're expressing it effectively to our mates. To prepare for this lesson, read 1 Corinthians 13:1–8; then read chapter 5 in *Marriage: From Surviving to Thriving*.

YOU ARE HERE

Imagine yourself sitting in a grand concert hall, dressed in your finest attire, waiting in eager anticipation as the musicians tune their instruments. The conductor strides across the platform to the applause of the crowd and mounts the stand. The ovation subsides as he raises his baton, and then . . .

Leader Help

By the end of this lesson, group members should understand the unique nature of *agape* as described by 1 Corinthians 13, evaluate how the love they express compares to *agape*, and fine new ways to show *agape* to their mates.

Nothing is complete without love. Unfortunately, we love too little and we love too seldom. So, on occasion, we need a gentle reminder of what it means to love someone with our whole hearts. That calls for wisdom and counsel from the Author of love.

—Marriage: From Surviving to Thriving

Leader Help

The "correct" answer to the questions that follow is implied in the introduction, so assure the members of the group that this is not a test. Encourage them to use this occasion to take stock of their priorities with shameless honesty. Have one or two brave volunteers elaborate on their answer with the group.

Nothing. No sound. No music. No performance. Nothing. The audience sits in silence, as does the orchestra. Then after an hour, the conductor turns, bows to the applause of the audience, and exits the stage. You stand up, gather your belongings, and leave the hall with the other patrons.

A concert without music? How absurd! Yet too many marriages are like that. Passionate, in-love feelings spark a romance; an affectionate friendship seasons the relationship; and the couple may even remain committed to the marriage until death. The external requirements are there, but without *agape*, marriage lacks the very quality God intends it to celebrate and display.

In a previous lesson, we discovered the central role of commitment, which will keep you and your partner in close proximity for a lifetime. But without *agape*, you cannot experience unity. *Agape* is the glue that every couple must diligently and delightedly apply.

Of the following qualities, which one do you value most in yourself?

❏ **Spiritual maturity**

❏ **Intelligence**

❏ **Selflessness/servant's heart**

❏ **Generosity**

❏ **Wisdom**

❏ **Ability to make others feel loved**

❏ **Faith**

❏ **Leadership skills**

❏ **Ability to communicate well**

❏ **Talent for teaching or speaking**

Why did you choose this as your primary quality?

Of the qualities in the list, which has the greatest potential to unite two people? Why?

Describe how you expressed your love for your mate when the relationship was new.

We may wield the powers of almighty God, yet if we don't possess His uniquely defining quality of love, we are nothing.

—*Marriage: From Surviving to Thriving*

What feelings did you experience during those early days?

Do you still experience those feelings, or have they changed or faded?

Leader Help

To add a unique dimension to this group meeting, try inviting an older married couple who demonstrates affection for each other and enjoys each other's company. Ask them to share how they met and the feelings they originally experienced. How did they maintain their warm feelings for one another after their "in-love" euphoria faded? Have them read 1 Corinthians 13 in advance and come prepared to comment on this description of love based on their experience.

DISCOVERING THE WAY

The beginning of a romance often involves feelings of incredible elation and an almost obsessive desire to seek the happiness of our lover. However, this is not love in the best sense of the word. Gary Chapman, author of *The Five Love Languages*, writes:

> The in-love experience does not focus on our own growth or on the growth and development of the other person. Rather, it gives us the sense that we have arrived and that we do not need further growth. We are at the apex of life's happiness, and our only desire is to stay there. Certainly our beloved does not need to grow because she is perfect. We simply hope she will remain perfect.[1]

Of course, people always need personal growth and development. But often for the first two years of a romance (on average), couples choose to ignore that obvious fact. When the "in-love" euphoria fades, what will take its place? What will keep the lovers bonded together as circumstances and emotions change? Fortunately, we get to decide. First Corinthians 13:1–8 tells us how.

The Priority of Love

The Greek language has at least three words that we translate into English as *love*. *Philos* describes affection between friends and family members. When Greeks thought of the love a man and a woman have for each other, they used the word *eros*. It comes closest to what we have described as the euphoric, in-love feelings that cause sparks to fly early in the romance. A third word, *agape*, was rarely used outside Jewish and Christian circles. It is this kind of love that Paul described in 1 Corinthians 13. Unlike the often short-lived *eros*, *agape* is the glue that couples must apply in order to maintain and enjoy a strong bond. One scholarly lexicon compares the terms well.[2]

Eros	*Agape*
A general love of the world seeking satisfaction wherever it can	A love which makes distinctions, choosing and keeping its object
Determined by a more or less indefinite impulsion toward its object [him or her]	A free and decisive act determined by its subject [self]
In its highest sense, is used of the upward impulsion of man, of his love for the divine	Relates for the most part to the love of God, to the love of the higher lifting up the lower
Seeks in others the fulfillment of its own life's hunger	Must often be translated "to show love"; it is a giving, active love on the other's behalf.

Read 1 Corinthians 13:1–4. Paul began his treatise on *agape* by establishing its priority over all other virtues. List in the space below the gifts and abilities he mentions in verses 1–3.

Every marriage needs a healthy does of *eros*—a passionate, emotional, lusty appetite for one another. But that's not the kind of love that holds a couple together. . . . Where *eros* is a mystery that evokes good feelings, *agape* is a choice that produces good character.

—*Marriage: From Surviving to Thriving*

Leader Help

To amplify this exercise, you may consider either reading the sections in *Marriage: From Surviving to Thriving* that define these terms. Or consider listening to the corresponding excerpt from the sermon "Essential Glue for Every Couple to Apply."

Choose any one of your answers above, and describe the character of someone who applies this gift without love.

How much respect would you have for this person?

Love in Action

We've seen that *agape* is the necessary glue for every couple, but what does it actually look like? How can we tell it apart from *eros*? In 1 Corinthians 13:4–7, Paul described *agape* using both positive statements ("love is") and negative terms ("love is not"). Let's take a closer look.

Read 1 Corinthians 13:4–7 carefully. Place the descriptions in the appropriate column.

Positive
(Love is/does . . .)

Negative
(Love is not/does not . . .)

These are the dos and don'ts of love, and they're topped off by a tall order in 1 Corinthians 13:7. Alfred Plummer summarized it well when he wrote, "When Love has no evidence, it believes the best. When the evidence is adverse, it hopes for the best. And when hopes are repeatedly disappointed, it still courageously waits."[3]

GETTING TO THE ROOT

In order to maintain proper English style, most English versions of the Bible translate some of the terms in 1 Corinthians 13:4–7 as adjectives. However, Paul uses verbs exclusively, describing *agape* as though he were describing the actions of a person. For instance, an extended paraphrase of "Love is patient, love is kind and is not jealous" might read, "Love counts to ten before responding, love adapts himself well to bring about good, and he does not zealously clutch."

The effect is twofold. First, Paul's description reinforces the point that love is not a noun, such as a feeling; love is a verb, an action. Love cannot be anything more than what it does. Second, his description encourages the reader to substitute his or her name for the word *love* each time it appears.

For Paul, *agape* is the intersection of truth, salvation, and obedience to God. And this is where your marriage and Christ meet.

—*Marriage: From Surviving to Thriving*

The following paraphrase of 1 Corinthians 13:4–7 expands the meaning of each Greek term to make it clear while retaining the spirit of Paul's style. A blank line replaces each occurrence of the term *agape*. Take the time to read it slowly and digest each phrase, and then write your name in the blank (in place of the English word *love*).

_____ counts to ten before responding,

_____ adapts himself/herself well to bring about good, and he/she does not zealously clutch.

_____ does not try to impress others with his/her speech and does not make himself/herself appear more noteworthy, does not behave shamefully, does not strive to obtain what he/she wants, does not jab back in response to irritation, does not keep a mental note of a wrong, does not celebrate because of an unrighteous or unjust deed, but instead celebrates with the truth.

_____ continually protects all things, completely trusts despite all things, unfailingly maintains confidence through all things, and remains utterly steadfast in all things.

As you filled your name in this paragraph, which statements felt like a bit of a stretch in your marriage relationship?

Love Never Fails

After describing *agape* in action, Paul introduced the next section of his treatise with the bold statement "Love never fails" (1 Corinthians 13:8). This is not meant to affirm the saying "Love conquers all." Neither does it suggest that when people fail, their love is not genuine. Given the context, a better rendering of the Greek would be, "Love never comes to an end."

According to 1 Corinthians 13:8, which of the following abilities will be obsolete in heaven? (Verses 9–12 provide additional clues.)

The ability to:

- ☐ speak for God (prophesy)

- ☐ teach or preach

- ☐ love others

- ☐ understand the universe

- ☐ trust without seeing

What impact should this awareness have on the daily life of a Christian?

Of the gifts listed above, which is the most celebrated in your home? In your church? What can you do to encourage emphasis on the correct priority?

Leader Help

If you chose to invite an older couple to the group meeting, ask them to prepare some examples of how they have been able to demonstrate *agape* to each other. Otherwise, divide the group into men and women and encourage the groups to brainstorm suggestions for how one might give tangible expression of *agape* to his or her mate.

STARTING YOUR JOURNEY

Love, just like glue, can create a lasting bond, but in order to be effective, it has to be applied. It won't do any good if it stays in the container. We discovered earlier that Paul used verbs to describe love. The same is true throughout the Bible; love without expression isn't love at all.

Entire books have been written on how to express love; one of the more notable is *The Five Love Languages: How to Express Heartfelt Commitment to Your Mate.*[4] In it, Gary Chapman outlines five different ways people give and receive love. We recommend it as a resource as you start your journey in this area. You may be surprised to find you've been expressing love in your own love language rather than your spouse's!

Applying the Glue

Below you'll find a few helpful principles to encourage you and help you get started. They may appear simple at first glance, but give them serious consideration. Sometimes we need to get back to basics.

1. *Write it down.*

Saying "I love you" to your spouse regularly is very important. When the stresses of life chip away at the self-esteem and joy of your mate, he or she needs to be reminded of your love. Seeing words of love and affirmation in writing can be powerfully comforting and just might be the strong reassurance of commitment that your mate needs.

Look for the "Heart to Heart" exercise at the end of this lesson to discover how you can make "writing it down" a regular part of your love affair with your spouse.

2. *Risk it often.*

Love and trust go together. We learned in lesson one that a result of the Fall is the fear of vulnerability. Sometimes we don't express love freely because we fear it will make us look foolish, or we'll do it poorly, or we'll experience rejection, or any number of other reasons.

Have you considered a particular expression of love toward your spouse but been too afraid to follow through? What kept you from expressing love freely to your mate?

How do you think your mate would respond if you admitted this to him or her?

 Describe a time when your partner took a risk to express his or her love for you.

How did your mate's effort make you feel?

How did this affect your love, admiration, or respect for your mate?

The likelihood that the person who promised to remain by your side regardless of the circumstances will ridicule or reject your sincere expression of love is probably very low. In fact, he or she may have similar fears about expressing love. It's true, you might not get the response you imagine, but your love is worth expressing. Discover the joy of giving love without expecting anything in return. Yes, love involves risk. As C. S. Lewis wrote, "The only place outside Heaven where you can be perfectly safe from all the dangers and perturbations of love is Hell."[5]

3. *Do it now.*

Never wait to express love. If we wait until the time is right, or when we feel better, or after the big project at work is complete, or once the stress has lifted, we will soon look back on a life of love that could have been. One songwriter put it this way: "Life is what happens to you while you're busy making other plans."[6]

After Senator Paul Tsongas was diagnosed with cancer, a friend wrote to him, affirming his decision not to run for reelection. We would do well to remember his sobering words: "No man ever said on his deathbed, 'I wish I had spent more time in the office.'"[7]

What reason do you have to delay expressing love to your mate before noon tomorrow?

HEART TO HEART

Take some time to put some of your thoughts in writing, preferably in your own handwriting rather than a printout. This is not nearly as difficult as it might seem. Start by answering these questions to spark your thinking.

What features or qualities first attracted you to your mate that you still enjoy and admire?

What are three things about your mate for which you are most thankful?

List three positive words that describe your mate.

When do you miss your mate the most?

What dreams or ambitions has your mate discussed with you? What can you say in support of them?

What has your mate done for you lately for which you are thankful?

What does your mate do regularly that you appreciate?

Once you have recorded some answers to these questions, compose a small note consisting of a few sentences that express a thought or two. Begin with an affirmation of your love, mention one or two items at the most, and close with an affirmation of your love.

Consider making this a habit. Take a small notebook and place one of the above questions at the top of each page. Once every couple of weeks, read the questions and fill in a few answers. This activity should come even easier to you if chose to follow through on the Heart to Heart exercise on pages 70–73 in lesson four. (Be sure to keep the notebook where your mate will not see it and spoil the surprise.) Write at least one note per week, and leave it where your mate will be surprised to see it: on the bathroom mirror, in his or her lunch bag, on the dashboard, in the sock drawer. Use your imagination to keep your mate guessing.

By examining the actions described in 1 Corinthians 13, in this lesson we learned the unique nature of *agape* as distinct from *eros*. How do your feelings or expressions of love compare to the essential glue that holds couples together? Have you found new ways to show *agape* to your mate? Have you made time to do them?

Notes

Notes

Notes

Lesson Six

What Families Need to Thrive

— Excerpts from Ephesians —

THE HEART OF THE MATTER

The family is where we learn our first lessons about life and how to relate with other people; it is where we should learn the difference between right and wrong, good and evil. Healthy families prepare us for marriage by modeling the skills necessary to enjoy intimacy in marriage. However, no family is perfect. Even the best, healthiest families can pass along destructive habits that undermine close relationships. We cannot underestimate the power of those early models to shape how we conduct ourselves in marriage.

Several passages in the latter half of Ephesians provide at least six habits that, if cultivated, will help reinforce healthy models of relating while keeping poor habits from repeating themselves in our marriages.

In preparation for this lesson, read Ephesians 4:25, 29–32; 5:21–22, 25; 6:1, 10–11, 18; then read chapter 6 in *Marriage: From Surviving to Thriving*.

YOU ARE HERE

If your childhood home were a museum of memories, what kinds of exhibits would it

Leader Help

By the end of this lesson, group members should know at least three characteristics of a healthy family, evaluate the influence of their family of origin on how they relate to each other in marriage, and commit to apply at least one new habit to their marriage as they avoid rehearsing old ones.

Marriage is God's invention, and He intended this lifelong, exclusive union between a man and a woman to become the foundation upon which a family is built. I am convinced that a strong marriage will cover a multitude of difficulties in other areas, while a struggling marriage will undermine most hopes of building a healthy household.

—*Marriage: From Surviving to Thriving*

showcase? Recollections of laughter and artifacts from a pleasant, winsome childhood? Or perhaps it would display episodes of pain, mistreatment, neglect, or abuse? Take a few moments now to revisit your museum of family memories.

HEART TO HEART

Reviewing your history with your mate can be a helpful way to understand why some things work in your household and others don't. The following are eight characteristics of a healthy family. Place an X on the line below each quality to indicate how well it was modeled in your family of origin. Then have your mate do the same with a different colored pen. Be sure to use this exercise as an opportunity not to place blame but to discuss your family background with your mate and to better understand each other.

1. *Commitment*. Family members were dedicated to living their lives in support of one another with unquestioned loyalty.

Almost never   Rarely   Sometimes   Usually   Nearly always

◄───────────────────────────────────►

2. *Quantity time*. Family members spent lots of time together and knew each other well.

Almost never   Rarely   Sometimes   Usually   Nearly always

◄───────────────────────────────────►

3. *Communication*. Each person in the family was allowed opportunity to discuss anything and ask any question without fear of condemnation or ridicule.

Almost never   Rarely   Sometimes   Usually   Nearly always

◄───────────────────────────────────►

4. *Problem solving.* The family pulled together during times of crisis and relied upon one another for support.

Almost never   Rarely   Sometimes   Usually   Nearly always

⟵————————————————————⟶

5. *Encouragement.* Expressions of affirmation and encouragement were frequent and natural.

Almost never   Rarely   Sometimes   Usually   Nearly always

⟵————————————————————⟶

6. *Spiritual commitment.* The family shared a commitment to knowing, loving, and serving the Lord.

Almost never   Rarely   Sometimes   Usually   Nearly always

⟵————————————————————⟶

7. *Trust.* Each member trusted the others and guarded the trust he or she had earned.

Almost never   Rarely   Sometimes   Usually   Nearly always

⟵————————————————————⟶

8. *Grace.* Each member enjoyed freedom to be different, to have weaknesses, and to fail without condemnation.

Almost never   Rarely   Sometimes   Usually   Nearly always

⟵————————————————————⟶

Work through the questions in the Heart to Heart feature of this chapter. In which areas did your family of origin excel?

In which areas did it not?

We're not looking to blame anyone, but we want to take a realistic inventory of the training we received in the art of marriage building. No family is perfect, so all of us can look back and find at least one characteristic that won't come naturally to us because we never saw it modeled, or we saw it modeled poorly.

—Marriage: From Surviving to Thriving

Leader Help

People have a need to tell their stories and to be understood. This exercise may open the floodgates of their pain. Encourage the members to keep the focus of their comments on *current* behavior patterns that resemble those modeled in their family of origin. They can keep their focus by asking the question, "How does this affect the way I treat my spouse?"

Leader Help

In preparation for this series of questions, the group leader may want to consult the fuller discussion of these six principles from chapter 6 of the book *Marriage: From Surviving to Thriving,* or as an alternative, play the appropriate section of the corresponding sermon.

 In what areas did your family of origin prepare you well for building an intimate marriage? Do those skills come naturally to you?

Without looking to lay blame on anyone else, how did your family of origin teach you poorly?

 ## DISCOVERING THE WAY

The book of Ephesians was originally intended to help unify a church. But the principles it contains are well suited to build a strong marital bond. Apply them to your marriage and the positive effects can be profound. And because the marriage is the nucleus of the home, whatever makes the marriage healthy will benefit the entire household.

Consider these six healthy habits as you examine the verses from which they come. As you do, evaluate which actions and attitudes come most naturally to you and which ones will require discipline to apply.

1. *Pursue truth.* Relationships are built on trust, and trust is built on truth.

In Ephesians 4:25, Paul wrote, "We are members of one another." What do you think he meant by this?

If being "members of one another" and truth go together, what does dealing in falsehood imply about the relationship?

2. *Exercise restraint and courtesy.* The tongue can quickly tear down what love so carefully builds.

 According to Ephesians 4:29, what should be the sole purpose for anything we say to our spouse? (Look up the definition of *edify* and/or *edification* in a dictionary for more insight.)

How well do you feel you apply the principle of Ephesians 4:29 in your marriage?

Do you do this better with people outside your family or inside? Why?

How would your spouse answer these questions about you?

 Ephesians 4:32 offers positive advice on how to build up your mate. What are the three adjectives listed in this verse?

Why do you think it's easier to be this way toward strangers than those closest to us?

The word translated "unwholesome" means rotten or putrid, which implies that certain speech has a contaminating effect on another. It's like slipping a rotten piece of meat into your mate's sandwich, or cooking for him or her an omelet contaminated with salmonella. Why would you want to destroy the internal health of someone you love so much?

—*Marriage: From Surviving to Thriving*

GETTING TO THE ROOT

"Let all bitterness . . . be put away from you"
EPHESIANS 4:31

The term translated "bitterness" in Ephesians 4:31 comes from a word meaning "sharp" or "pointed" like an arrow. The figurative Greek expression works much like ours. "Let all sharpness be put away from you." In this case, Paul describes a spirit that refuses to reconcile long-standing sentiments. Each treasured offense is like a porcupine's quill—the more you have, the pricklier you feel to others, even when you don't mean to be.

---

3. *Learn to cooperate and adapt*. Jesus Christ, the supreme ruler of all, became the servant of all.

 According to Ephesians 5:21, who is supposed to be submissive, or subject, to whom?

4. *Demonstrate Christlike love*. This kind of love inspires adaptation and cooperation in others.

Explain how the command in Ephesians 5:25 is a manner of submission.

Submission is a tough word to use these days because we don't like the idea of being subservient to anyone. Yet Jesus Christ, the creator and ruler of everything, became a servant to all. Leadership in the home is the husband's responsibility. And if we take our example from Christ, we find that He led His disciples from a kneeling position. The husband leads his wife by laying down his desires and needs in order to fulfill hers.

DIGGING DEEPER

The principle of headship and submission not an arbitrary structure that changes with the times but an established order consistent with God's own relationship with the world. The relationship between God the Father and His Son, Jesus Christ, demonstrates this beautiful dynamic. The Father, Son, and Holy Spirit are eternal and equal in their power and deity (John 1:1; 5:18; 17:5). However, each has a specific role in His work in creation.

The Gospels tell us that the Son voluntarily subjects His will to the Father's (Luke 22:42; John 5:30; 17:11). Paul taught that this ordered relationship between the Father and the Son should be mirrored in an ordered relationship between husbands and wives (1 Corinthians 11:3). Men and women are equal in their human nature and value, while at the same time the wife should voluntarily accept the headship of her husband and the husband should voluntarily love his wife and take the role of godly leadership in his family.

> If men take the lead in demonstrating Christlike love—the duty we are so quick to neglect—all of the areas of life we feel so compelled to dominate would delight to rest in our leadership.
>
> —*Marriage: From Surviving to Thriving*

5. *Show respect for authority.* Showing respect for parents will help create a peaceful marriage. When one or both partners struggle with authority issues, strife between them is inevitable. Respect for parents translates into

respect for the boss, respect for the law, respect for church leadership, ultimately respect for the Lord. And because each married partner has a certain amount of authority over the other, refusal to respect authority can quickly divide them.

How can you fulfill the command in Ephesians 6:1 as a married couple? Be specific about your situation.

6. *Stand strong against the real enemy.* Satan will take advantage of any opportunity you leave to him.

Marital conflict can cause you to feel as though your spouse is your enemy. But, according to Ephesians 6:10–11, who is your real enemy?

How can he keep you fighting the wrong enemy?

Ephesians 6:18 offers two commands to help us fight the real enemy. What are they?

How often do you pray about your marriage—when things are going great, or only in a crisis? Do you actively pray against deception, Satan's chief weapon? If not, now's the time to start. Pray for a clear vision of what's going on in your family, what difficulties your spouse is facing, what changes your children are enduring.

In the space below, write the names of each of your family members and list specific prayer requests for each. Then pray about them, preferably with your spouse!

Persevering in prayer can help you stay alert to potential problems before they arise. As you do, it is critical that you pay attention to what's going in your family's and your spouse's world. The enemy would like nothing more than to see you and your spouse move gradually toward isolation due to apathy, laziness, or busyness. (We'll talk more about marital erosion in the next chapter.) Author Dennis Rainey lists some warning signs:

- A feeling that your spouse isn't hearing you and doesn't want to understand;

- An attitude of, "Who cares?" "Why try?"

- "Tomorrow we'll talk about it—let's just get some sleep";

- A feeling of being unable to please or meet the expectations of your spouse;

- A sense that he's [or she's] detached from you;

- A feeling that [he's or] she's going [his or] her own way;

- A refusal to cope with what's really wrong: "That's *your* problem, not mine";
- A feeling that keeping the peace by avoiding the conflict is better than the pain of dealing with reality.[1]

Do you notice any of these tendencies creeping into your marriage or your attitude about your spouse? If so, which ones?

Handling difficulties promptly is your best defense against your adversary. Don't allow them to go unattended.

STARTING YOUR JOURNEY

At the beginning of the lesson, we listed six principles of a healthy family. Then we discovered six habits from Ephesians 4–6 that can build a greater sense of unity in marriage. As you take an honest look at your marriage, chances are good you are already doing some of them. Keep it up! Chances are also good that you're repeating some unhealthy patterns from your family of origin. Applying some of the biblical principles in this chapter to help correct those patterns will not come naturally, but they will be worth the trouble.

Habits and mind-sets that have been engrained in you since childhood will be hard to counter, but remember, the goal is to improve your marriage and cultivate intimacy. Every feeble step toward that goal counts. Keep at

Leader Help

You might consider reproducing the below chart on a large writing board. Encourage the group to elaborate on how they see the principles in action.

it! Try focusing on just one of the habits that doesn't come as naturally to you as you complete this section.

 Review each of the six principles in the previous section and indicate which qualities of a healthy family it directly affects.

		Principles					
		Pursue truth	Exercise restraint and courtesy	Learn to cooperate and adapt	Demonstrate Christ-like love	Show respect for authority	Stand against the real enemy
Qualities	Commitment						
	Quantity Time						
	Communication	✓					
	Problem-solving	✓					
	Encouragement						
	Spiritual Commitment	✓					
	Trust	✓					
	Grace						

Highlight or place an asterisk on the left side of the chart next to the qualities that come least naturally to you. (They may or may not match up with those scoring low in the Heart to Heart exercise earlier.) Where are you weakest? Which principles from Ephesians will require focused attention? These will be your greatest challenge.

In this workbook, we have often referred to your spouse as your "partner." This is one instance in which we use the term more literally. You are not in this alone. Reveal your weakness to your partner, apologize for any harm or neglect for which you are responsible, and solicit his or her help in making the appropriate changes. Devise a plan for how you can work together. Don't expect your mate to do this exercise in return. Make this your responsibility, and allow the Holy Spirit to influence your spouse.

This level of vulnerability may be difficult for you. In lesson four, we suggested an exercise to help cultivate complete honesty (see page **70**). Review the exercise and put it to use here. You may be surprised to see your mate respond to your vulnerability with unusual tenderness. This is yet another exercise in trust.

In this lesson, we saw several characteristics of a healthy family and realized that, without exception, all of us need to work on relating to each other in marriage. Rehearsing old habits learned from our own parents can become the "default" mode in which our current marriages operate. But with commitment, old habits can be replaced with new ones. Will you start today?

Notes

Notes

Notes

Lesson Seven

Danger Signs of Marital Erosion

— 1 Samuel 1–4 —

THE HEART OF THE MATTER

Erosion is an insidious problem that attacks a home silently, slowly, subtly, and steadily to destroy what people carefully build. And it can happen to anyone. Fortunately, erosion can be stopped before it does too much harm if we address the problem early with decisive action. To prepare for this lesson, read 1 Samuel 2:12–4:22; then read chapter 7 in *Marriage: From Surviving to Thriving*.

YOU ARE HERE

The citizens of a small town just north of Pittsburgh proudly cut the ribbon on a brand-new red-brick township building. They had been careful with their planning and diligent during construction. The architecture, engineering, and craftsmanship were superb, and the project had gone very well. Soon the police department and other city offices were enjoying their new space.

Within a few weeks, however, doors began to stick and windows wouldn't open and close quite as easily as before. Then, ominous cracks began to form over the doorways and in the corners of the rooms. Before long, a

Leader Help

By the end of this lesson, group members should recognize the four danger signs of domestic erosion, seriously consider that it may be occurring in their marriage, and commit to responding with decisive action sooner rather than later.

large crack was discovered in the mortar, running along the foundation and up two stories. Bricks were coming loose. Eventually the building was completely lost to a subtle, mysterious, and destructive force.

Despite the sound engineering and the excellent efforts of the construction crew, a controversial coal-mining process, known as longwall mining, had been used to remove earth deep beneath the structure. Its foundation had no support! The same had been happening to several historic buildings around the area. The resulting erosion broke a once-sound structure into pieces.

What can happen to a building can happen to a marriage. Fortunately, the danger signs appear early, and, if we take them seriously and respond decisively, we can keep the relationship strong and sound. Take a few minutes to inspect your marriage for signs of domestic erosion.

Leader Help

If group members have not answered these questions on their own prior to the meeting, give time for them to do so, and then encourage them to share the results. Through group interaction, some members will remember time commitments that others have forgotten, so a few may need to adjust their figures. You might want to bring a calculator to the meeting!

 About how many hours a week does it take to sufficiently maintain a healthy marriage relationship?

If you are employed, how many hours each week do you work away from your family, including the time you commute? (a) _____

If you bring work home with you, how many hours each week do you work at home? (b) _____

If you travel, how many days per week, on average, are you gone? Multiply this by 24. (c) _____

Estimate how many hours you spend meeting the needs of your children or on their activities. (d)

_____

Estimate how many hours you spend on hobbies, reading, exercise, church activities, or other pursuits that don't involve your mate. (e) _____

Each week has approximately 112 waking hours. Let's assume 12 hours each week are spent on miscellaneous, unforeseen activities, leaving 100 hours each week.

Place your answers in the following formula:

100

− _____ (a)

− _____ (b)

− _____ (c)

− _____ (d)

− _____ (e)

= _____ (result)

This is a rough estimate of the time you have currently available to devote exclusively to your marriage.

Compare this number to the number of hours you suggested are necessary to maintain a healthy marriage relationship. What do you notice?

Do you feel you have sufficient time each day with your partner to talk about the day's events? Do you have enough opportunity for special times together? How would your spouse answer?

Consider how you and your partner spend the time you have together. What do you usually do? What do you wish you did?

 What are the subtle signals your mate sends when he or she is unhappy or experiencing difficulty? How sensitive are you to these? You may need to consult him or her on this.

When you sense that something is wrong with your mate or with your relationship, how do you typically respond? Do you take decisive action?

If you could change something about your relationship with your mate, assuming anything were possible, what would you change?

DISCOVERING THE WAY

First Samuel 1–4 records the story of Eli and the domestic erosion that destroyed his home. The story does not involve his marriage. In fact, a wife is never mentioned. However, the manner in which he conducted his relationship with his two sons, Hophni and Phinehas, helps us to see exactly what *not* to do in all of our relationships. Tragically, far too many husbands and wives unwittingly follow Eli's pattern and later react with surprise to find their homes crumbling around them.

A Domestic Erosion Observed

If you haven't already done so, read 1 Samuel 2:12–4:22 before answering the following questions. The story was originally intended to introduce Samuel by way of contrast to Eli, who represents the religious climate of Israel at the time, and the two sons, who personify the hearts of the Hebrew people. For our purposes, pay particular attention to the relationship between this father and his sons.

DOORWAY TO HISTORY

After Israel had settled in the Promised Land and Joshua had died, the nation had no king. The Lord raised up strong leaders from among the people to

Leader Help

Examining the life of someone in the Bible whose flaws overshadow his accomplishments can lead to a simplistic view of the man. Help the group members empathize with Eli in order to see life from his perspective. He could have just as easily been a busy megachurch pastor as an ancient priest.

carry out the duties of a king, only without all the royal frills. These were called "judges," from which the book of the Bible derives its name. At any given time, the duty might be shared by several judges, each governing a region. This system was first established by Moses (Exodus 18:13–26), to whom God gave strict instructions concerning conduct and justice (Deuteronomy 16:18–20; 17:2–13).

The role of judge was to lead the nation in foreign affairs, including war and diplomacy. He (or in one case, she) would also oversee the construction of cities, roads, and other civic projects, as well as hear cases brought by citizens seeking justice. The traditional place for this was by the city gate.

The context of this story tells us that Eli was not only the high priest of Israel but also a judge for forty years (1 Samuel 4:18). He was a very busy father.

 According to 1 Samuel 1:3, what position did Hophni and Phinehas hold?

What does Deuteronomy 17:12–13 suggest about the power of their occupation and influence they wielded?

What does 1 Samuel 2:12–13 say about their character?

Were they competent to do the job? Who was to prepare them for service?

What sins did Hophni and Phinehas commit in verses 12–17?

Based on your reading, how would you evaluate Eli's morality and integrity? What was his relationship with the Lord like?

The Crisis (The Result)

First Samuel 2:18–21 tells us that some time passed before the events of verse 22. Samuel grew up while Eli grew old. Apparently, the sins taking place in the tabernacle grew as well.

First Samuel 2:22 describes a new dimension to the sins of Hophni and Phinehas. What were their crimes?

What does 1 Samuel 2:22–25 say that Eli did to correct his sons?

According to Leviticus 20:10, what should have happened to Eli's sons?

GETTING TO THE ROOT

First Samuel 2:24 says, "No, my sons; for the report is not good which I hear the LORD's people circulating." This translation is faithful to the original language, but it fails to convey the extent to which the scandal had spread. The key word is based on the Hebrew verb *abar*, which usually describes the spatial movement of something, "to pass over, to move across, to travel through." And the form of the word is causative, meaning that someone or something is inciting the action.

Everywhere Eli went, people were talking about the outrageous sins of his sons. Their deeds had caused reports to spread all across the nation so that their father could go nowhere without hearing about it. What had started as a tiny crack, a small infraction of the rules, had gradually become a national emergency. The Lord's temple had been corrupted, the covenant compromised, and the very character of God called into question.

According to Deuteronomy 21:18–21, what should have happened to Hophni and Phinehas after ignoring their father's rebuke? What did happen?

⚥

In the written account of that episode, a clue suggests that Eli had moved from passive bystander to active participant. Eli didn't personally steal meat from the worshipers, but his expanding girth suggested that he savored every morsel at the dinner table.
                —*Marriage: From Surviving to Thriving*

Considering their crimes, what was wrong with Eli's words in 1 Samuel 2:24–25?

Eli received three separate warnings concerning his sons (1 Samuel 2:22; 2:27–36; 3:10–18). At each warning, the story tells us something about Samuel as well (1 Samuel 2:21; 2:26; 3:1). While the children of Eli spun out of control, Samuel grew taller, wiser, and godlier. God patiently waited for Eli to take action and, in the meantime, prepared a way to restore the integrity of His tabernacle.

Given the severe warnings he received (1 Samuel 2:29–32), why do you think Eli chose to remain passive about his sons' immoral behavior?

How would you describe Eli's attitude in verse 3:18?

How would you have responded if someone said to you what Samuel told Eli in 1 Samuel 3:10–15?

The Danger Signs of Erosion

All marriages will experience difficulty, sin, poor communication, and any number of problems. These are not necessarily danger signs; they occur in every family. The danger signs appear in how we respond. Eli's response to the growing crisis in his family and in the tabernacle reveals four danger signs.

Too Busy.

Eli held positions of both high priest and judge. As Alexander Whyte comments:

Away back, at the beginning of his life, Eli had taken far too much in hand. Eli was not a great man like Moses or Aaron, but he took both the office of Moses and the office of Aaron upon his single self. Eli was both the chief judge and the high priest in himself for the whole house of Israel. The ablest, the most laborious, the most devoted, the most tireless and sleepless of men could not have done what Eli undertook to do. . . .

And, taking up what was beyond mortal power to perform, the certain result was the he did nothing well.[1]

Too Dull.

He remained insensitive to the early words of warning he received from the people and from the unnamed prophet. Perhaps too busy to intervene before the sins became grievous, he found it easier to become callous than to face them.

Too Slow.

He waited too long to correct his sons. By the time Eli rebuked Hophni and Phinehas, they had become entrenched in their sins. They regarded their father and his God with bitter cynicism.

Too Easy.

When he did confront his sons, Eli's words in 1 Samuel 2:22–25 were not appropriate for the seriousness of their sins. These should have been the first words he spoke upon seeing the very first, minor infraction of the rules. His action was woefully inadequate, perhaps because he could not bring himself to do what was right.

Leader Help

Most of the questions in this section are for personal reflection and evaluation rather than group interaction. However, read the three exhortations and then consider allowing the group to break into couples to work through the questions and answers together as well as the Heart to Heart feature. As a group, each couple may summarize what they learned about themselves and their marriage or how they have chosen to respond to what they learned.

 STARTING YOUR JOURNEY

Difficulties will certainly challenge our marriages, and responding will require awareness and toughness—awareness to see the signs early and toughness to do what may be difficult. Sometimes the solution isn't obvious. To avoid the paralysis that confusion can cause, consider three brief exhortations from our study.

1. *Wake up!*

Even the most intelligent and thoughtful people can overlook needs at home. Often this is because we are too busy and in too much of a hurry to notice subtle clues. Nevertheless, an occasional message will break through just enough to catch our attention. We stop in our tracks long enough to ask, "Was that something?" only to shake it off with, "It was nothing."

When you next have a moment like that, stop. Ask. Listen. Check it out. Then give the matter your complete attention.

2. *Talk straight!*

Marriage experts are unanimous in their recommendation for problem solving: communication is crucial. After effective listening, straight talk is the most difficult aspect to master. This is the art of speaking to be understood rather than to make a point. Straight talk breaks down when either person stops trying to understand the other.

Thinking back over the past week, how much conversation with your mate was for the purpose of learning something new or seeking to understand a perspective?

For what purpose are most of your conversations with your mate?

A special word to men:

Gentlemen, communication is to a woman what physical intimacy is to you. When you stop talking and listening, she is no less wounded than you would be if she were to suddenly rebuff your advances and tell you that you are no longer desirable to her. Yes, it's that important, and it's that dangerous to the health of your relationship.[2]

3. *Stay close!*

Meaningful conversations usually take place when we are relaxed and thinking beyond the immediate. While it is healthy to plan regular times of communication with your spouse, sometimes the best conversations occur at the most unlikely times and have profound impact on the health of the marriage. Because some things cannot be planned, we must provide them ample opportunity.

 Do you have enough time with your mate to enjoy easy, casual conversation, or do you spend most of your time together talking about problems or practical matters?

If you were given three hours of time exclusively to communicate with your spouse, would you know where to start? Come up with a couple of creative questions that could open the door to transparency. Consider asking about your spouse's passions, hopes and dreams for the

Most situations require tenderness; however, some demand toughness. By "tough" I don't mean harsh. Toughness is the willingness to do what is personally hard to do. When we are willing to do what is right, despite the great personal cost, our real priorities are revealed.

—*Marriage: From Surviving to Thriving*

future, or special memories from the past. Have fun brainstorming on this one! Write your questions below.

 HEART TO HEART

Time is the currency of our age. If we are to have sufficient time for meaningful conversations and the intimacy that results, and if we are to arrest problems before they become crises, we must have ample time with our mates. Just like everything else in life, this will require planning and effort.

On the chart on the following page, shade in the blocks of time during which you or your mate is already currently committed. Each of you should use a different color to label the commitment.

If you are like most couples, you will not find many free spaces, so you will have to make some sacrifices, use creative thinking, or both.

What blocks of time remain for you and your mate to enjoy easy conversation? Mark these with a big circle or highlighter.

What time commitments can you release in order to have more time together?

How drastic are you willing to be in order to safeguard this time? What if this means reducing your involvements at church, cutting some of the time you spend on your own hobbies or social engagements, or even taking a lower salary (and consequently moving to a less expensive residence or downgrading your transportation)? Just how valuable is this time to you? To your marriage?

	Mon	Tues	Wed	Thur	Fri	Sat	Sun
5 am–6 am							
6 am–7 am							
7 am–8 am							
8 am–5 pm							
6pm–7 pm							
7 pm–8 pm							
8 pm–9 pm							
9 pm–10 pm							
10 pm–11 pm							
11 pm–12 pm							

Domestic erosion is not inevitable except for the unaware and the unwise. Perhaps nowhere else is the old adage more appropriate than marriage: "An ounce of prevention is worth a pound of cure." Wake up, talk straight, and stay close.

All buildings have small cracks, creaking doors, and sticky windows from time to time. These are not nearly as important as how we respond to them. The danger signs appear in how we take action when those subtle problems begin to occur—and they certainly will.

—*Marriage: From Surviving to Thriving*

Though erosion in our marriage and family often works beneath the surface, there are danger signs that—if present in your life—can almost guarantee that hidden erosion is taking place. Are you too busy? Too insensitive toward the needs of your spouse? Too slow to resolve conflict? Too easy on problems? Commit to responding with decisive action now . . . because tomorrow may be too late.

Notes

Notes

Notes

Lesson Eight

Staying Young As Your Family Grows Older –
— Joshua 14:6–14 —

THE HEART OF THE MATTER

A person with a negative attitude often drags others into his or her slough of despond, which not only is no fun at parties but can utterly destroy a marriage. How we respond to the inevitable difficulties and challenges of life will shape how we approach marriage, how we face difficulties with a partner, and how we cope with the challenges of aging. The example of Caleb provides no fewer than three specific attitude choices that contribute to having an infectious exuberance for life, which will keep a marriage youthful even as we grow older.

In preparation for this lesson, read Joshua 14:6–14; then read chapter 8 in *Marriage: From Surviving to Thriving*.

YOU ARE HERE

Difficulties, like unwelcome houseguests, never seem to leave as soon as we hope. And the longer they stay, the more likely they are to rob our household of joy and enthusiasm for life. They can even wear down an otherwise strong marriage.

By the end of this lesson, group members should accept that the attitudes and habits of today will determine the marriage they will have tomorrow, recognize some common negative attitudes, and resolve to cultivate the three qualities that gave Caleb an infectious exuberance for life.

137

Leader Help

Negative attitudes can become such an invisible part of our demeanor that we don't recognize how often they enter our conversation. To illustrate this tendency, start the session by handing each member five pieces of candy, such as chocolate kisses or peppermints. Then challenge each person to be on the lookout for negative statements, cynicism, sarcasm, self-pity, or any other expression of a negative attitude as the class continues. Encourage them to be kind but strict! Anyone showing evidence of a negative attitude must surrender a candy for each infraction, and let the group decide by majority vote if there is any controversy. Give a small prize to the people left with the most candies at the end of your time together.

Lingering difficulties often cause these common negative attitudes:

1. A Sense of Uselessness

This is an attitude that says, "I'm no good to anybody. I'm just in everybody's way. Why am I still around?" When difficulties keep us pinned to the ground, productivity seems impossible, so it's natural to doubt our self worth. If someone is especially given to performance-based love and acceptance, this attitude can be particularly debilitating.

2. Self-Pity

This attitude says, "Nobody cares about me. Why should I bother reaching out to anyone? If anyone really cared, they'd come to me." Self-pity leads to blame, which turns to bitterness. And bitterness pushes others away, reinforcing the self-pity. This destructive cycle will destroy a marriage like cancer unless it is addressed aggressively.

3. Fear

People who are obsessed with fear have an attitude that says, "I've been hurt too many times, and I can't afford to be hurt again. I must avoid risk and be proactive in protecting myself." Unfortunately, fear turns the danger we hope to avoid into a reality. By recoiling from life and love, we voluntarily give up the very things we fear to lose.

4. Inappropriate Remorse

This attitude is forever looking back over its shoulder with a deep, heavy sigh, saying, "If only I hadn't _____. If only I had _____." Regret is a healthy response to poor choices in the past. Remorse, however, combines regret with a dreadful sense of guilt causing what

Merriam-Webster describes as "a gnawing distress arising from a sense of guilt for past wrongs: self-reproach."[1]

Once a sin has been forgiven by God, guilt for that wrong has no place in the believer's life. We learned in Lesson One that the sin of Adam and Eve, and the appropriate guilt they felt, alienated each of them from God and from each other. Sin and guilt have the same effect on us. However, the mission of Jesus Christ is that of reconciliation. He took our guilt upon Himself, leaving us none to bear. If you are a believer in Jesus Christ, remorse has no place in your life and you have no reason to withdraw from the Lord or your mate.

 Can you think of a real-life example of a person you have known who is characterized by one of these four negative attitudes? Describe this person and how you and others respond to such a person.

Leader Help

The purpose of this is to illustrate the attitudes, not to disparage others. Members should avoid naming individuals and try to come up with examples from their youth or distant past rather than recent people or people other members would know.

Which of these four attitudes are you most prone to adopt? If none, what other negative attitudes do you find at work in you most often?

The cares and challenges of life can beat you down, leaving little energy to invest in a marriage, to say nothing of enjoying it. You might be thinking that once better days come, you can do that. Unfortunately, you'll be waiting a long time. . . . The years you could have enjoyed are gone.

—*Marriage: From Surviving to Thriving*

Describe how this negative attitude affects your relationship with your partner. If possible, give an example.

How have you tried to combat this attitude in the past? How successful were you?

How can your partner best respond when you struggle with this attitude?

DISCOVERING THE WAY

Caleb had more reasons than most to complain. He was criticized for his unwavering belief in God's promises. The unfaithfulness of his countrymen caused him to suffer punishment he didn't deserve. Though Caleb clearly exhibited stronger leadership skills than anyone, God chose Joshua instead. Caleb's dream of claiming the Promised Land had to wait forty-five years, during which he buried most of his peers. Yet, somehow, a youthful exuberance kept him on the frontiers of faith, ready for any challenge.

The books of Numbers and Joshua contain the story of this "original mountain man" and the qualities that made him remarkable—qualities we can make our own.

An Old Testament Hero With Attitude

Caleb first appears in Numbers 13 as one of twelve spies sent by Moses to scout the Promised Land (verses 1–20). They spent forty days in Canaan gathering information, and then Moses gathered the nation for a report (verses 27–33).

 Read Numbers 13:27–33. Those who held the majority opinion included specific reasons for turning back. What were they?

Who was the chief spokesman for the view that Israel should take the land?

What reason did Caleb offer for taking the land?

The Anakim (the people of Anak) were enormous people. . . . These were the basketball players and football linemen of their day. Imagine facing . . . an army of Shaquille O'Neals (340 pounds, standing seven foot one).

—*Marriage: From Surviving to Thriving*

Caleb's opinion could be characterized as brash or naive, yet we know it was neither. How do you explain his confidence? (see Numbers 14:6–9).

According to Numbers 14:10, how did the other leaders respond?

Because the people of Israel chose to follow the majority report, God punished the nation for their lack of faith. He sentenced them to a nomadic, homeless life in the wilderness south of Canaan for forty years—enough time for the unbelieving generation to die off. However, the Lord promised to preserve Caleb and Joshua so that they would enjoy the inheritance they were ready to claim.

During the forty years of wilderness wandering and the ordeals the nation faced—including the multiple thousands of funerals—we hear nothing about Caleb. His story resumes in Joshua 14 after Israel had entered the land.

Joshua had successfully led the invasion of Canaan, and the Hebrew people had broken the inhabitants' ability to resist them. However, the job was far from done. The land was to be divided among the twelve tribes, with each tribe responsible for defeating the remaining armies, taking the cities, and expelling the inhabitants as God had ordered. When the time came for the land to be parceled out, Caleb stepped forward with a bold speech, recounting his faithfulness to God and God's promises and ending with a strong reassurance of his vigor even at age eighty-five. He concluded with, "Give me this hill country about which the LORD spoke on that day . . . I will drive them [the inhabitants] out as the LORD has spoken" (Joshua 14:12).

Qualities That Add Up to a Great Attitude

Caleb possessed at least three qualities worth emulating that combined to give him an attitude of can-do enthusiasm. He had these three qualities at age forty, and they fueled his fire at age eighty-five.

1. An Unconditional Devotion to the Lord

 Read Joshua 14:6–14. A phrase appears three times (in slightly altered form) in the story. Look for it in verses 8, 9, and 14. What is it?

GETTING TO THE ROOT

Behind the New American Standard Bible's rendering of "I followed the LORD fully" is a quirky Hebrew clause. The Hebrew word behind the adverb *fully* is actually a verb, and an intense form of the verb at that. So the literal translation would be, "I filled [completely] after the LORD my God." This is an idiomatic expression to say, "What the Lord left for me to do, I completed with my whole self." One lexicon describes this intense use of *to fill* as "completely, formally, fill, i.e., do something with an attitude or feeling of great and earnest dedication."[2]

2. *An Unwavering Belief in God's Word*

 In verse 10, what gave Caleb the right to claim Hebron and the hill country as his inheritance?

How do you think this influenced his confidence?

Review Numbers 14:6–8. Do you notice any change in Caleb's perspective in Joshua 14:12?

3. *Humility*

Caleb made three bold claims in Joshua 14— one in verse 8, one in verse 11, and another in the latter half of verse 12. List them below.

Does Caleb's speech seem arrogant or proud to you? Why or why not?

Once Moses died, Joshua stood in the spotlight of history, while Caleb remained in the shadows. Do you see evidence of envy, bitterness, or spite in Caleb's attitude?

Remember that humility is not having a poor self-image. Humility is regarding others as more important than self.
—*Marriage: From Surviving to Thriving*

These three qualities—unconditional devotion to the Lord, an unwavering belief in God's Word, and humility—all combine to give Caleb an irrepressible attitude of fortitude. In his speech, he boldly said, "Give me this hill country." The Hebrew term translated "hill country" is the singular word for *mountain*. The context tells us that Caleb's claim included Hebron and the entire region around it, so his word choice probably carried a double meaning, referring to the land and to something else. A clue to the full breadth of his request can be found in the report in Numbers 13.

Looking once again at the unfaithful spies' report in Numbers 13:28–29, whom did they fear most?

Their territory was both rugged and prosperous; difficult to capture, but worth the fight. As with most challenges, great reward requires great risk.

—*Marriage: From Surviving to Thriving*

The giant Anakim (or descendants of Anak), the Amalekites, the Jebusites, and quite possibly the Hittites all lived in the region promised to Caleb. Caleb likely intended his choice of the word *mountain* to be metaphorical as well as literal. "Give me this challenge!"

Caleb made good on his big talk. With the Lord's promise in hand, "Caleb drove out from there the three sons of Anak: Sheshai and Ahiman and Talmai, the children of Anak. Then he went up from there against the inhabitants of Debir" (Joshua 15:14–15). Finally, after forty-five years of waiting, Caleb was able to claim the land he was promised and to share in the covenant with the God he loved and served fully.

STARTING YOUR JOURNEY

We, too, can determine to cultivate Caleb's attitude of fortitude. As we seek to make his qualities our own—unconditional devotion to the Lord, an unwavering belief in His Word, and humility—five key statements will help us apply them to life. The result will undoubtedly be a positive attitude that sees opportunity behind each difficulty. You'll be more fun to live with, and your marriage will remain young as your family grows older.

From your present perspective, what is the greatest difficulty or challenge you face as you look to the future? What concerns you most about your marriage as you and your spouse age?

Keeping your answer in mind, consider these five statements—five facts—and contemplate how they might impact your situation. If you're fortunate enough to have very few difficulties at this time, fortify yourself for the future. How might these affect your perspective and attitude?

1. Your mind never gets old—*keep exercising it.*
2. Your life is not over—*keep enjoying it.*
3. Your strength is not gone—*keep developing it.*
4. Your opportunities have not vanished—*keep pursuing them.*
5. Your God is not dead—*keep seeking Him.*

 As you reflect on your current struggles, which of these five statements resonates within you? How could a shift in attitude affect your situation?

Leader Help

As with many applications in this series, some of these questions may bring up personal issues. The leader should be prepared with his or her own answers, or ask a couple of others in the group to share if they are comfortable. Encouraging and exhorting others to apply these principles, or hearing from those who have done so already, will go a long way toward motivating commitment in these areas.

I am convinced that these will keep your marriage vibrant and fun (even when you're still chasing each other around that assisted-living home in wheelchairs)!

—*Marriage: From Surviving to Thriving*

I challenge you to take a different approach to your marriage, starting now. I challenge you to square off against whatever difficulties you might be facing, not with daredevil recklessness, but with fresh enthusiasm and in complete dependence upon your God.

—Marriage: From Surviving to Thriving

HEART TO HEART

The human mind is a paradoxical machine. God created it with remarkable powers. It seeks to create order out of chaos, sifting through untold amounts of data to retain the significant while ignoring the unimportant. It then arranges the information into neat, predictable categories. New information causes an amount of stress to the brain. Until everything is brought into equilibrium, it exists in an agitated, excited state.

The paradox is this: the brain craves new information; it requires a certain amount of chaos in order to stay healthy. When we experience nothing new, the brain has no other choice but to recycle the old information over and over. The inevitable results are boredom, a preoccupation with all that is wrong in the world, a sense of hopelessness, and a host of negative attitudes.

This can be deadly for a marriage.

Fortunately, the answer is both simple and fun: *change the scenery*. This can involve something drastic, such as changing where you live, or something as simple as taking a day off to explore a place new together. Usually, it isn't until something negative occurs that we allow change to jar ourselves from our routines, making change feel synonymous with pain. Why not introduce a pleasant change on your own terms?

Plan a day, preferably during the week, when you and your mate can be without children, work, or any other responsibility. Choose someplace close-by that neither of you has experienced. A museum, the zoo, a nearby town known for its antique shops, a nature trail—whatever either one of you might enjoy. The place and the activity are not nearly as important as the need to experience new sights, sounds, smells, and flavors as a couple.

Talk about anything you like, even old problems if that occurs naturally. The change in scenery will give your old perspectives a new light. You might think of new solutions or find the courage to try something bold. Or you might choose to keep the conversation light so you can focus on just having fun together. The point is to change the scenery and allow your minds (and your developing sense of adventure!) to take care of the rest.

Schedule one of these days at least once every three or four months, and you will be delighted by the difference it produces in your attitude and your relationship.

Your attitudes affect your habits—and your habits influence your attitude. Both determine the kind of marriage you'll have. In this lesson, we saw that certain negative attitudes and actions are common in marriage—and they can also be fatal. However, if we exercise our minds, enjoy our lives, develop our strength, pursue new opportunities, and seek God first, we'll stay young at heart, even as our families grow older. Are you ready to take your marriage with a great attitude?

How to Begin a Relationship with God

The book *Marriage: From Surviving to Thriving* and this companion volume take as their primary subject matter the mysterious union of a husband and wife. Indeed, this is the most significant person-to-person relationship any married person will experience. However, no human relationship can be more important than our relationship with God.

The most marvelous book in the world, the Bible, tells us how we can know and enjoy God with four vital truths. Let's look at each truth in detail.

OUR SPIRITUAL CONDITION: TOTALLY CORRUPT

The first truth is rather personal. One look in the mirror of Scripture, and our human condition becomes painfully clear:

> There is none righteous, not even one;
> There is none who understands,
> There is none who seeks for God;
> All have turned aside, together they have become useless;
> There is none who does good,
> There is not even one. (Romans 3:10–12)

We are all sinners through and through—totally corrupt. Now, that doesn't mean we've committed every atrocity known to humankind. We're not as *bad* as we can be, just as *bad off* as we can be. Sin colors all our thoughts, motives, words, and actions.

Look around. Everything around us bears the smudge marks of our sinful nature.

Despite our best efforts to create a perfect world, crime statistics continue to soar, divorce rates keep climbing, and families keep crumbling.

Something has gone terribly wrong in our society and in ourselves, something deadly. Contrary to how the world would repackage it, me-first living doesn't equal rugged individuality and freedom; it equals death. As Paul said in his letter the Romans, "The wages of sin is death" (Romans 6:23)—our emotional and physical death through sin's destructiveness, and our spiritual death from God's righteous judgment of our sin. This brings us to the second truth: God's character.

GOD'S CHARACTER: INFINITELY HOLY

Solomon observed the condition of the world and the people in it and concluded, "Vanity of vanities! All is vanity" (Ecclesiastes 1:2; 12:8). The fact that we know things are not as they should be points us to a standard of goodness beyond ourselves. Our sense of injustice in life on earth implies a perfect standard of justice elsewhere. That standard and source is God Himself. And God's standard of holiness contrasts starkly with our sinful condition.

Scripture says that "God is Light, and in Him there is no darkness at all" (1 John 1:5). He is absolutely holy—which creates a problem for us. If He is so pure, how can we who are so impure relate to Him?

Perhaps we could try being better people, try to tilt the balance in favor of our good deeds, or seek out wisdom and knowledge for self-improvement. Throughout history, people have attempted to live up to God's standard by keeping the Ten Commandments or living by their own code of ethics. Unfortunately, no one can come close to satisfying the demands of God's law (Romans 3:20). So, what can we do?

OUR NEED: A SUBSTITUTE

Here we are, sinners by nature, sinners by choice, trying to pull ourselves up by our own bootstraps and attain a relationship with our holy Creator. But every time we try, we fall flat on our faces. We can't live a good enough life to make up for our sin, because God's standard isn't "good enough"—it's perfection. And we can't make amends for the offense our sin has created without dying for it.

Who can get us out of this mess?

If someone could live perfectly, honoring God's law, and would bear sin's death penalty for us—in our place—then we would be saved from our predicament. But is there such a person? Thankfully, yes!

Meet your substitute—*Jesus Christ*. He is the One who took death's place for you!

> [God] made [Jesus Christ] who knew no sin to be sin on our behalf, so that we might become the righteousness of God in Him. (2 Corinthians 5:21)

GOD'S PROVISION: A SAVIOR

God rescued us by sending His Son, Jesus, to die for our sins on the cross (1 John 4:9–10). Jesus was fully human and fully divine (John 1:1, 18), a truth that ensures His understanding of our weaknesses, His power to forgive, and His ability to bridge the gap between God and us (Romans 5:6–11). In short, we are "justified as a gift by His grace through the redemption which is in Christ Jesus" (Romans 3:24). Two words in this verse bear further explanation: *justified* and *redemption*.

Justification is God's act of mercy, in which He declares believing sinners righteous, while they are still in their sinning state. Justification doesn't mean that God *makes* us righteous, so that we never sin again, rather that He *declares* us righteous—much like a judge pardons a guilty criminal. Because Jesus took our sin upon Himself and suffered our judgment on the cross, God forgives our debt and proclaims us *pardoned*.

Redemption is God's act of paying the ransom price to release us from our bondage to sin. Held hostage by Satan, we were shackled by the iron chains of sin and death. But, like a loving parent whose child has been kidnapped, God willingly paid the ransom for you. And what a price He paid! He gave His only Son to bear our sins—past, present, and future. Jesus's death and resurrection broke our chains and set us free to become children of God (Romans 6:16–18, 22; Galatians 4:4–7).

OUR RESPONSE: FAITH IN CHRIST

These four truths describe how God has provided a way to Himself through Jesus Christ. Since the price has been paid in full by God, we must respond to His free gift of eternal life in total faith and confidence in Him to save us. We must step forward into the relationship with God that He has prepared for us—not by doing good works or being a good person but by coming to Him just as we are and accepting His justification and redemption by faith.

> For by grace you have been saved through faith; and that not of yourselves, it is the gift of God; not as a result of works, so that no one may boast. (Ephesians 2:8–9)

We accept God's gift of salvation simply by placing our faith in Christ alone for the forgiveness of our sins. Would you like to enter a relationship with your Creator by trusting in Christ as your Savior? If so, here's a simple prayer you can use to express your faith:

Dear God,

I know that my sin has put a barrier between You and me. Thank You for sending Your Son, Jesus, to die in my place. I trust in Jesus alone to forgive my sins, and I accept His gift of eternal life. I ask Jesus to be my personal Savior and the Lord of my life. Thank You.

In Jesus's name, amen.

If you've prayed this prayer or one like it and you wish to find out more about knowing God and His plan for you, contact us at Insight for Living. You can speak to one of our pastors on staff by calling the number or writing to us at the address below.

Insight for Living
P.O. Box 269000
Plano, TX 75026-9000
1-800-772–8888

Notes

Lesson 1: This Is Not Your Grandfather's Family
Unless otherwise noted, all material in this chapter is based on or quoted from "This Is Not Your Grandfather's Family," a sermon by Charles R. Swindoll, 22 August 2004, and chapter 1 of the *Marriage: From Surviving to Thriving* book by Charles R. Swindoll.

Lesson 2: Getting Back on Target
Unless otherwise noted, all material in this chapter is based on or quoted from "Getting Back on Target," a sermon by Charles R. Swindoll, 29 August 2004, and chapter 2 of *Marriage: From Surviving to Thriving* book by Charles R. Swindoll.

1. Frank and Mary Alice Minirth, *Secrets of a Strong Marriage* (Colorado Springs: Cook Communications, 2005), 122–23. Copyright © 2005 by Frank and Alice Minirth. Used with permission by Cook Communications Ministries. To order, www.cookministries.com. All rights reserved.
2. R. Laird Harris, Gleason L. Archer, Jr., and Bruce K. Waltke, eds., *Theological Wordbook of the Old Testament*, vol. 1 (Chicago: Moody, 1980), 30.
3. Harris, Archer, and Waltke, eds., *Theological Wordbook of the Old Testament*, 75.
4. *The American Heritage Dictionary of the English Language*, 4th ed. Copyright © 2000 by Houghton Mifflin Company, s.v. "value." Accessed online. All rights reserved.

Lesson 3: Symphony of Survival in the Key of "C"

Unless otherwise noted, all material in this chapter is based on or quoted from "Symphony of Survival . . . in the Key of 'C'," a sermon by Charles R. Swindoll, 12 September 2004, and chapter 3 of the *Marriage: From Surviving to Thriving* book by Charles R. Swindoll.

Lesson 4: Practical Advice on Making a Marriage Stick

Unless otherwise noted, all material in this chapter is based on or quoted from "Practical Advice on Making a Marriage Stick," a sermon by Charles R. Swindoll, 19 September 2004, and chapter 4 of the *Marriage: From Surviving to Thriving* book by Charles R. Swindoll.

1. Dale Carnegie, *How to Win Friends and Influence People*, rev. ed. (New York: Pocket Books, 1982), 50.
2. John R.W. Stott, *The Message of Ephesians*, The Bible Speaks Today Series (Downers Grove, IL: InterVarsity, 1979), 185.

Lesson 5: Essential Glue for Every Couple to Apply

Unless otherwise noted, all material in this chapter is based on or quoted from "Essential Glue for Every Family to Apply," a sermon by Charles R. Swindoll, 12 December 2004, and chapter 5 of the *Marriage: From Surviving to Thriving* book by Charles R. Swindoll.

1. Gary Chapman, *The Five Love Languages: How to Express Heartfelt Commitment to Your Mate* (Chicago: Northfield, 1995), 33–34.
2. Gerhard Kittel, ed., *Theological Dictionary of the New Testament*, ed. and trans. Geoffrey W. Bromiley, vol. 1 (Grand Rapids: Eerdmans, 1987), 37.
3. A.T. Robertson and Alfred Plummer, *A Critical and Exegetical Commentary on the First Epistle of St. Paul to the Corinthians*, 2d ed. (Edinburgh: T. & T. Clark, 1914), 295.
4. Gary Chapman, *The Five Love Languages: How to Express Heartfelt Commitment to Your Mate* (Chicago: Northfield, 1995).
5. C. S. Lewis, *The Four Loves* (New York: Harcourt, Brace, & World, 1960), 169.
6. John Lennon, "Beautiful Boy (Darling Boy)," *Double Fantasy* (Geffen Records, 1980).
7. Anna Quindlen, *A Short Guide to a Happy Life* (New York: Random House, 2000).

Lesson 6: What Families Need to Thrive

Unless otherwise noted, all material in this chapter is based on or quoted from "What Families Need to Succeed," a sermon by Charles R. Swindoll, 13 February 2005, and chapter 6 of *Marriage: From Surviving to Thriving* by Charles R. Swindoll.

1. Dennis Rainey, *Staying Close: Stopping the Natural Drift Toward Isolation in Marriage* (Dallas: Word, 1989), 15. Reprinted by permission. Copyright © 1989 by Dennis Rainey. W Publishing, a division of Thomas Nelson, Inc., Nashville, Tennessee. All rights reserved.

Lesson 7: Danger Signs of Marital Erosion

Unless otherwise noted, all material in this chapter is based on or quoted from "Dangers of Domestic Erosion," a sermon by Charles R. Swindoll, 20 February 2005, and chapter 7 of *Marriage: From Surviving to Thriving* by Charles R. Swindoll.

1. Alexander Whyte, *Bible Characters*, vol. 1 (London: Oliphants Ltd., 1959), 217.
2. Shaunti Feldhahn, *For Women Only: What You Need to Know About the Inner Lives of Men* (Sisters, OR: Multnomah, 2004), 92.

Lesson 8: Staying Young As Your Family Grows Older

Unless otherwise noted, all material in this chapter is based on or quoted from "Staying Young As Your Family Grows Older," a sermon by Charles R. Swindoll, 27 February 2005, and chapter 8 of *Marriage: From Surviving to Thriving* by Charles R. Swindoll.

1. *Merriam-Webster's Collegiate Dictionary*, 10th ed., s.v. "remorse."
2. James Swanson, *Dictionary of Biblical Languages with Semantic Domains: Hebrew*, Old Testament (Bellingham, WA: Logos Research Systems, 1997), electronic ed.